My Life with Charlie Brown

PEANUTS.
by SCHULZ

NO, I THINK HE'S WRITING..

Edited and with an introduction by M. Thomas Inge

CHARLES M. SCHULZ

My Life with Charlie Brown

University Press of Mississippi / Jackson

www.upress.state.ms.us

Designed by Todd Lape

The University Press of Mississippi is a member
of the Association of American University Presses.

Manufactured in the United States of America

First printing 2010
∞
Library of Congress Cataloging-in-Publication Data

Schulz, Charles M. (Charles Monroe), 1922–2000.
  My life with Charlie Brown / Charles M. Schulz ; edited
and with an introduction by M. Thomas Inge.
      p. cm.
  Includes index.
  ISBN 978-1-60473-447-8 (alk. paper)
1. Schulz, Charles M. (Charles Monroe), 1922–2000.
2. Cartoonists—United States—Biography. 3. Schulz,
Charles M. (Charles Monroe), 1922–2000. Peanuts.
I. Inge, M. Thomas. II. Title.
  PN6727.S3Z46 2010
  741.5′6973
  [B 22]   2009033756

British Library Cataloging-in-Publication Data available

On behalf of Sparky
this book is dedicated to

his wife, Jeannie

and his children
Meredith
Monte
Craig
Amy
and
Jill

Contents

Introduction

Charles Monroe Schulz, better known as "Sparky" among his family and friends, was twentieth-century America's favorite and most highly respected cartoonist. His comic strip, *Peanuts*, appeared daily in over two thousand newspapers in the United States and abroad in a multiplicity of languages. Compilations of the strips sold in millions of copies during his lifetime and often topped best seller lists, and more recently a series of volumes collecting the complete run of *Peanuts* appeared in the *New York Times* listings.

Thousands of toy and gift items bore and continue to bear the likenesses of Charlie Brown, Lucy, Snoopy, and the other characters who populate their world. A stage musical based on *Peanuts*—*You're a Good Man Charlie Brown*—has remained one of the most frequently performed shows in American theatrical history, and several award-winning animated television specials continue to be shown annually and sold in DVD. Even today, almost a decade after the untimely death of Schulz on February 12, 2000, classic *Peanuts* reprints continue to hold their own space in major newspapers throughout the United States and in other countries.

While sometimes bewildered by the enormous influence of the characters of his creation on American culture in general, Schulz held to a principle of integrity in the comic strip itself. Beginning with the first strip published on October 2, 1950, until the last published on Sunday, February 13, 2000, the day after his death, Schulz wrote, penciled, inked, and lettered by hand every single one of the daily and Sunday strips to leave his studio, 17,897 in all for an almost fifty-year run. No other single cartoonist has matched this achievement, but that is not what remains important about *Peanuts*.

While cultural mavens have seldom granted the lowly comic strip aesthetic value, Schulz moved his feature in an artistic direction that was minimalist in style but richly suggestive in content. Any piece of art that endures, no matter the form or medium, draws on the cumulative traditions that have preceded it, and in turn reshapes and reinvigorates those traditions with new life and relevance for the future. Schulz did exactly that in *Peanuts*. His comic strip drew on a rich history of creative accomplishments in graphic humor and comic art and ultimately revived the comic strip as a relevant form that spoke to readers for the remainder of the twentieth century. He demonstrated its versatility in dealing with the social, psychological, and philosophical tensions of the modern world.

Charlie Brown and his friends were preoccupied with what has possessed and continued to obsess all of us—the relationship of the self to society, the need to establish our separate identities, anxiety over our neurotic behavior, and an overwhelming desire to gain control of our destinies. Charlie Brown appeals to us because of his resilience, his ability to confront and humanize the impersonal forces around him, and his unwavering faith in his ability to improve himself and his options in life. In his insecurities and defeats, his affirmations and small victories, Charlie is someone with whom we can identify. Through him we can all experience a revival of the spirit and a healing of the psyche. This has been Charles Schulz's amazing gift to the world through his small drawings appearing daily in the buried pages of the comic section of the newspaper. He was for the second half of the twentieth century our major pop philosopher, therapist, and theologian, and unlike Lucy's booth, his shingle was always up.

In addition to his finely honed skills as a graphic artist, Schulz was also adept with the written word. Although he never fancied himself as a writer, and would normally rely on the cartoon image in conjunction with the word to convey his meaning, when given the opportunity, he produced a clear and straightforward prose that was admirable in its style and simplicity. He was frequently asked to give a talk or speech, produce an article for a magazine or newspaper, write an autobiographical essay for one of his anthologies, or comment on his chosen profession as a cartoonist. When he did so, the outcome was more often than not insightful and engaging in quality, and probably more revealing than anything anyone else has written about him and his work.

Schulz's major prose writings, both published and unpublished, have been gathered in this volume. Here the reader will learn, directly from the man himself, the facts of his early life and the development of his career. Here he talks about a wide variety of topics: the sources of his creativity and inspiration, how *Peanuts* came to be, the meaning of each character in the strip, his daily routine, how to do a chalk talk, how to achieve a career in cartooning, and the importance of his work in animation and television. There is a good deal here, as well, on a personal note: his work ethic, his philosophic attitude, and his religious beliefs which changed over time, until he would eventually call himself a "secular humanist." His theories of humor emerge as well, as in his essay "On Staying Power":

> If you are a person who looks at the funny side of things,
> then sometimes when you are lowest, when everything seems
> totally hopeless, you will come up with some of your best ideas.
> Happiness does not create humor. There's nothing funny about
> being happy. Sadness creates humor.

Despite the obvious depth of thought and maturity of attitude in *Peanuts*, Schulz did not consider himself an intellectual. Although he finished high school, he was largely a self-educated man who read widely and deeply in the great ideas and literature of the world. He was surprised when critics and college professors expressed interest in his work, but he held his own in conversations and interviews with them when they visited his studio to pay homage. He seemed to be regretful that he had not gone to college himself, and he greatly respected the academic and intellectual life. In the spring of 1965, Schulz signed up for a course in the novel at Santa Rosa Junior College under Professor Cott Hobart. As Schulz described the experience in his essay "Don't Give Up":

> I took a college course in the novel a few years ago, and oddly enough I got an A in it. When I was a kid, I was a lousy student, the way Peppermint Patty is. I never knew what was going on, never did my homework, never did the reading assignments. This time I did all the reading and wrote a paper on Katherine Anne Porter's book *Pale Horse, Pale Rider*. As I wrote it, I pretended I was writing for *The New Yorker*. Afterwards the professor said to me, "I just want you to know that this is a perfect example of what a paper should be."

That essay appears in this collection for the first time in an appendix. Another unusual item included is a poem that Schulz wrote for his second wife Jeannie, she believes around 1980. This is the only poem found among his literary remains.

Not included are the numerous prefaces, introductions, jacket blurbs, and brief comments he obligingly wrote for fellow cartoonists and friends in their published books. His papers also include notes and comments that did not find their way into his completed essays. Here are two examples:

> One of the most disturbing elements in today's living is what most of us describe as the average workman's lack of pride in craftsmanship. We are surrounded with luxury, and yet constantly outraged by breakdowns in things we have purchased. If there were but one bit of advice I could give to a young

person, it would be to learn to do at least one task well. Following that, I would say also, don't sell out to the baser elements of your profession. Do what you do on a high plain. I am proud to say that in a period when books dealing with every sort of perversion seem to be flooding the market, we sold over 800,000 copies of *Happiness Is a Warm Puppy*, a book without guile, a book of innocence. If God has given you a talent, do not use it ungratefully.

When I finish the last drawing of the day and drop the pencil in the tray, put down the pen and brush and put the top on the ink bottle, it always reminds me of the dentist when he puts his instruments down on the tray and reaches to turn off the light.

One of them borders on the metaphysical:

I remember the time we all went somewhere, but I don't know where it was. We had a good time, but I don't remember what we did, because it was a long time ago.

The intent of this collection of Schulz's essays is to round out the portrait of the man as he saw himself. His measure has been taken in several biographies, none of which seem satisfactory to those who remember the man and his work differently. That is the fate of all prominent people, especially in an age of celebrity. He speaks entirely for himself in these pieces, and the reader can experience to some degree directly the greatness of his mind and soul.

Editorial changes have been minor, mainly correcting errors in spelling or grammar. The essays are given their published titles, although Schulz may not have been the source. Unpublished essays have been given titles by the editor. Original place of publication is noted after each item.

The editor wishes to thank Jeannie Schulz for encouraging this project from the start. The task would have been more difficult without the thoughtful assistance of the staff at the Charles M. Schulz

Museum and Research Center at Santa Rosa, California, Karen Johnson, Director. Knowing Schulz himself gave me a special advantage, and I remain grateful for his friendship. The help of my student research assistant at Randolph-Macon College, Rachelle Phillips, has been invaluable. A Mednick Memorial Fellowship awarded by the Virginia Foundation for Independent Colleges made an essential research trip possible. President Robert R. Lindgren and the administration at Randolph-Macon College continue to provide a supportive and enthusiastic working environment. As always and not least, with Donária, all things are possible.

—M. THOMAS INGE
March 2009

Chronology

1922   Charles Monroe Schulz, the only child of German born barber Carl Schulz and his wife Dena Halverson Schulz, is born on November 26 in Flat No. 2 at 919 Chicago Avenue, South in Minneapolis, Minnesota. An uncle nicknames Charles "Sparky" after the horse Sparkplug in the comic strip *Barney Google*.

1928   The family resides on James Avenue in St. Paul when Charles attended kindergarten at Mattocks School where a teacher encouraged his first drawings.

1934   The Schulz family acquires a black and white mutt named Spike, later an inspiration for Snoopy.

1936   The family resides at 473 Macalester Street in St. Paul when Charles entered St. Paul Central High School and worked as a caddie at Highland Park Golf Club.

1937   Schulz's first published drawing is a sketch of Spike contributed to the February 22 panel of the newspaper comics feature *Believe It or Not* by Robert Ripley.

1940   Schulz graduates from high school, and although he contributes drawings to the senior yearbook, they are not published.

1941   Schulz signs up for a correspondence course in cartooning offered by Federal Schools (later known as Art Instruction, Inc.) of Minneapolis.

1943   Dena Schulz, his mother, dies of cancer. Drafted into the Army during World War II, Schulz serves with the Twentieth Armored Division in France and Germany as an infantryman, staff sergeant, and machine gunner.

1945   Discharged by the Army, he returns to St. Paul, is hired to letter comic book pages for the Roman Catholic publication *Timeless Topix*, and becomes an instructor for Art Instruction, Inc. Schulz lives with his father in an apartment above his barbershop on the corner of Snelling and Selby Avenues.

1947   He begins to contribute a cartoon feature called *Li'l Folks* to the St. Paul *Pioneer Press* where it runs weekly for two years.

1948   Schulz sells a panel cartoon to the *Saturday Evening Post*, where sixteen more of them would appear through 1950.

1950   Assembling a group of his *Li'l Folks* cartoons, Schulz sends them to United Features Syndicate, who invites him to New York where he signs a contract to develop a comic strip. On October 2, the first *Peanuts* daily strip appears in seven newspapers. He lives at 5521 Oliver Avenue, North in Minneapolis.

1951   Schulz marries Joyce Halverson (no relation to his mother's family) on April 18, and they would have five children: Meredith, Charles Monroe (Monte), Craig, Amy, and Jill. His father Carl marries his second wife, Annabelle. Schulz moves his family to Colorado Springs, Colorado, but returns the following year to Minneapolis.

1952   A *Peanuts* Sunday page begins on January 6, the strip appears in over 40 U.S. papers, and the first anthology, *Peanuts*, is published by Rinehart.

1955   Schulz is awarded the profession's highest honor, the Reuben (named after Rube Goldberg), by the National Cartoonists Society.

1958   With *Peanuts* in 355 U.S. papers and 40 foreign dailies, he is declared Humorist of the Year by Yale University. The Schulz family moves to 2162 Coffee Lane, Sebastopol, California.

1960   The National Education Association gives Schulz the School Bell Award. The first Hallmark greeting cards featuring *Peanuts* characters are released.

1962   *Happiness Is a Warm Puppy* by Schulz is published by Determined Productions. The National Cartoonists Society names *Peanuts* the Best Humor Strip of the Year.

1963   Anderson College in Anderson, Indiana, awards Schulz an honorary LHD degree.

1964   Robert L. Short's *The Gospel According to Peanuts* is published by John Knox Press. A second Reuben is awarded to Schulz by the National Cartoonists Society.

1965   *Peanuts* appears on the front cover of the April 9 issue of *Time* magazine. *A Charlie Brown Christmas*, a television special, wins both Emmy and Peabody awards.

1966   Schulz receives an honorary Doctor of Humane Letters degree from St. Mary's College in Moraga, California. Carl, his father, dies from a heart attack while visiting in

California from Minnesota. The Schulz family residence burns to the ground, as did Snoopy's doghouse in *Peanuts*.

1967   The Art Directors Club of New York awards Schulz a Certificate of Merit. *Peanuts* appears on the cover of the March 17 issue of *Life* magazine. The musical *You're a Good Man, Charlie Brown* opens off-Broadway on March 7 for a four-year run, and it would become the most frequently performed musical in American theatrical history. Governor Ronald Reagan of California declares May 24 Charles Schulz Day.

1968   Robert L. Short's *The Parables of Peanuts* is published by John Knox Press. Snoopy is assigned to the Manned Flight Awareness Program.

1969   The astronauts on Apollo X carry Snoopy and Charlie Brown into space with them. *Peanuts* appears on the cover of the April 12 issue of the *Saturday Review*. The Redwood Ice Arena in Santa Rosa, California, is built by his wife, Joyce, and opens on April 28.

1970   *Charlie Brown and Charlie Schulz* by Lee Mendelson and Schulz is published by World Publishing Company.

1971   June 17 is declared *Peanuts* Day in San Diego and Schulz is given the Key to the City. Snoopy publishes *It Was a Dark and Stormy Night* with Holt, Rinehart, and Winston. *Peanuts* appears on the cover of the December 27 issue of *Newsweek*, and Snoopy joins the Holiday on Ice show. *Peanuts* appears in more than 1,100 newspapers reaching a daily reading audience of over 100 million people.

1972   Schulz is divorced from Joyce Halverson.

1973   Schulz marries Jean Forsyth (Jeannie) on September 23. He builds a studio complex at 1 Snoopy Place in Santa Rosa, California, adjacent to the Redwood Ice Arena. He receives the Big Brother of the Year Award. *A Charlie Brown Thanksgiving*, a television special, brings an Emmy Award to Schulz as the writer.

1974   Schulz is named Grand Marshall of the Tournament of Roses Parade in Pasadena.

1975   *Peanuts* appears in 1,480 newspapers in the U.S. and another 175 throughout the world. *Peanuts Jubilee: My Life and Art with Charlie Brown and Others* by Schulz is published by Holt, Rinehart and Winston. *You're a Good Sport, Charlie Brown*, a television special, wins an Emmy Award.

1976   *Happy Anniversary, Charlie Brown*, a television special, wins an Emmy Award.

1978   Schulz is named Cartoonist of the Year by the International Pavilion of Humor in Montreal.

1979   *Happy Birthday, Charlie Brown*, by Lee Mendelson and Schulz is published by Ballantine Books.

1980   Schulz himself receives the Charles M. Schulz Award from United Feature Syndicate for contributions to the field of cartooning. *Charlie Brown, Snoopy, and Me* by Schulz and R. Smith Kiliper is published by Doubleday. *Life Is a Circus, Charlie Brown*, a television special, receives an Emmy Award.

1983   *What Have We Learned, Charlie Brown?*, a television special, wins a Peabody Award. Camp Snoopy opens at Knott's Berry Farm in Buena Park, California.

1984   *Peanuts* is sold to its 2,000th newspaper and achieves a place in the *Guiness Book of World Records*.

1985   *You Don't Look 35, Charlie Brown* by Schulz is published by Holt, Rinehart and Winston. The Oakland Museum in California opens an anniversary exhibition, *The Graphic Art of Charles Schulz*, and publishes the catalog.

1986   He is inducted into the Cartoonist Hall of Fame by the Museum of Cartoon Art and given its "Golden Brick" award for lifetime achievement.

1989   A biography, *Good Grief: The Story of Charles M. Schulz* by Rheta Grimsley Johnson, written with the cooperation of Schulz, is published by Pharos Books.

1990   The French Ministry of Culture awards Schulz the *Odre des Arts et des Lettres* in Paris, and the Louvre opens its exhibition *Snoopy in Fashion*. The National Museum of History in Washington, D.C., opens its exhibition, *This Is Your Childhood, Charlie Brown—Children in American Culture*.

1992   The Montreal Museum of Fine Art opens an exhibition, *Snoopy, the Masterpiece*. The Italian Minister of Culture awards Schulz the Order of Merit.

1994   *Around the World in 45 Years: Charlie Brown's Anniversary Celebration* by Schulz is published by Andrews and McMeel.

1995   *Around the Moon and Home Again: A Tribute to the Art of Charles M. Schulz* is held at the Space Center in Houston in celebration of the 45th anniversary of *Peanuts*. An A & E television biography is devoted to *Charles Schulz—A Charlie Brown Life*.

1996   A star is placed in honor of Schulz on the Hollywood Walk
        of Fame.

1997   The world premiere of *Peanuts Gallery* by composer Ellen
        Taaffe Zwilich is held at Carnegie Hall.

1999   *Peanuts* is selected as the best comic strip of the century
        second only to George Herriman's *Krazy Kat* in a survey of
        critics and comic artists by the *Comics Journal*. *Peanuts: A
        Golden Celebration* by Schulz is published by Harper Collins.
        You're a Good Man, Charlie Brown opens in a new production
        on Broadway. The International Museum of Cartoon Art in
        Boca Raton, Florida, opens a year-long celebration of the
        comic strip with an exhibition, *Fifty Years of Peanuts: The
        Art of Charles M. Schulz*.

2000   The last *Peanuts* daily appears on January 3 and the last Sun-
        day on February 13. On the evening of February 12, Schulz
        dies at his home in Santa Rosa. The Milton Caniff Lifetime
        Achievement Award is presented to Schulz posthumously
        by the National Cartoonists Society. Schulz is also awarded
        the Congressional Gold Medal, the body's highest civilian
        honor.

MY
LIFE

Li'l Folks

BY SPARKY

"You moved!"

"Happy birthday to you . . .
"Happy birthday to you . . .
"Happy birthday, dear . . .
"What did you say your
   name was?"

"Y'know, if you
were sure that you and
I were going to the
same high school, I'd
ask you to the senior
prom."

"No, no, no! . . . You don't seem to
understand!"

My Life and Art with Charlie Brown and Others

And so, 25 years have gone by. At one strip per day, that comes to almost 10,000 comic strips. Actually, this is not so much when you consider the longevity of many other comic features. Employees receive wristwatches if they have put in this much time with a company, but a comic-strip artist just keeps on drawing. (Somehow a comic-strip artist is never regarded as an employee.) I have been asked many times if I ever dreamed that *Peanuts* would become as successful as it is, and I think I always surprise people when I say, "Well, frankly, I guess I did expect it, because, after all, it was something I had planned for since I was six years old." Obviously I did not know that Snoopy was going to go to the moon, and I did not know that the phrase "happiness is a warm puppy" would prompt hundreds of other such definitions, and I did not know that the term "security blanket" would become part of the American language; but I did have the hope that I would be able to contribute something to a profession that I can say now I have loved all my life.

It is important to me, when I am discussing comic strips, to make certain that everyone knows that I do not regard what I am doing as Great Art. I am certainly not ashamed of the work I do, nor do I apologize for being involved in a field that is generally regarded as occupying a very low rung on the entertainment ladder. I am all too aware of the fact that when a reviewer for a sophisticated journal wishes to downgrade the latest Broadway play, one of the worst things he can say about it is that it has a comic-strip plot. This is also true for movie reviewers, but I tend to believe that movies, as a whole, really do not rank that much higher than comic strips as an art form. The comic strip can be an extremely creative form of endeavor. On its highest level, we find a wonderful combination of writing and drawing, generally done by one writer. But there are several factors that work against comic strips, preventing them from becoming a true art form in the mind of the public. In the first place, they are reproduced with the express purpose of helping publishers sell their publications. The paper on which they appear is not of the best quality, so the reproductions lose much of the beauty of the originals. The artist is also forced to serve many masters—he must please the syndicate editor, as well as the countless editors who purchase his comic strip. The strip is not always exhibited in the best place, but is forced to compete on the same page with other strips that may be printed larger or enjoy a better position. And there are always annoying things like copyright stickers, which can break up the pleasing design of a panel, or the intrusion of titles into first panels in order to save space. The true artist, working on his canvas, does not have to put up with such desecrations.

There is a trend these days to try to prove that comic strips are true art by exhibiting them in galleries, either for people simply to enjoy viewing, or for customers to purchase. It seems to me that although this is a laudable effort, it is begging the question, because how we distinguish something doesn't matter nearly as much as the purpose it serves. The comic strip serves its purpose in an admirable way, for there is no medium that can compete with it for readership or for longevity. There are numerous comic strips that have been enjoyed by as many as 60 million readers a day, for a period of fifty years. Having a large audience does not, of course, prove that something is necessarily good, and I subscribe to the theory that only a creation that speaks to succeeding generations can truly be labeled art. Unfortunately, very few comic strips seem to do this.

In my earliest recollections of drawing I seem to be at a small blackboard with a paper roller at the top on which are printed the ABC's. It was from this roller that I was able to learn the alphabet before I began kindergarten, and I know that I drew constantly on the blackboard and had it for many years.

It may have been on the first day at kindergarten, or at least during the first week, when the teacher handed out big crayons and huge sheets of white wrapping paper and told us to lie on the floor and draw something. Several of my mother's relatives had recently moved from Twin Cities to Needles, California, and I had heard my mother reading a letter from one of them telling of the sandstorms in Needles and also describing the tall palm trees. So when the teacher told us to draw whatever came to our minds, being familiar with the Minnesota snowstorms I drew a man shoveling snow, but then added a palm tree to the background.

I recall being somewhat puzzled when I was drawing the snow shovel because I was not quite sure how to put it in proper perspective. I knew that drawing the shovel square was not right, but I didn't know how to solve the problem. At any rate, it didn't seem to bother the teacher. She came around during the project, looked down at my drawing, and said, "Someday, Charles, you're going to be an artist."

I never knew what family problems caused us to make the move, but in 1930, when I was six years old, my mother and father and I drove from St. Paul to Needles in a 1928 Ford. I believe the trip took us almost two weeks. We remained in Needles for almost a year and I suppose there were some happy times, but I think my dad was disillusioned with what he saw. He had intended to continue northwest and settle in Sacramento, but somehow he never made the final move. After a year, we moved back to St. Paul and he repurchased his barbershop. I have memories of the trip to Needles, but I don't remember a single thing about the return trip to St. Paul. We settled in a neighborhood about two blocks from my dad's barbershop and most of my playtime life revolved around the yard of the grade school across the street from our apartment. In the wintertime we played in the deep snow, and in the summertime we either played baseball in the schoolyard or used its sandy wastes as the Sahara Desert when inspired by seeing movies such as *The Lost Patrol* with Victor McLaglen.

I was drawing cartoons during those years but created very few original characters. Most of the time I copied Buck Rogers or Walt Disney figures, or some of the characters in *Tim Tyler's Luck*. I was fascinated by the animals in this feature.

Early influences on my work were many. I continued to be a great fan of all the Disney characters when I was in grade school, and I also enjoyed Popeye and Wimpy very much. I used to decorate my loose-leaf binders with drawings of Mickey Mouse, The Three Little Pigs, and Popeye, and whenever friends in class would see these cartoons, I would be asked to draw them on their notebooks as well. I used to buy every Big Little Book and comic magazine that came out and study all of the various cartoonists' techniques. When I reached high school age, the work of Milt Caniff and Al Capp influenced me considerably, as well as that of some of the earlier cartoonists such as Clare Briggs ("When a Fella Needs a Friend"). I also thought there was no one who drew funnier and more warm-hearted cartoons than J. R. Williams. But the man who influenced me the most was Roy Crane with his drawings of Wash Tubbs and Captain Easy. His rollicking style laid the groundwork for many cartoonists who followed him. A book collection of *Krazy Kat* was published sometime in the late 1940s, which did much to inspire me to create a feature that went beyond the mere actions of ordinary children. After World War II, I began to study the *Krazy Kat* strip for the first time, for during my younger years I never had the opportunity to see a newspaper that carried it.

Also in my high school years, I became a Sherlock Holmes fanatic and used to buy scrapbooks at the local five-and-dime and fill them with Sherlock Holmes stories in comic-book form. A friend of mine named Shermy was one of my faithful readers, and when I started *Peanuts* I used his name for one of the original characters.

My scholastic career got off to a good start when I was very young. I received a special diploma in the second grade for being the outstanding boy student, and in the third and fifth grades I was moved ahead so suddenly that I was the smallest kid in the class. Somehow, I survived the early years of grade school, but when I entered junior high school, I failed everything in sight. High school proved not much better. There was no doubt I was absolutely the worst physics student in the history of St. Paul Central High School. It was not until I became a senior that I earned any respectable grades at all. I have often felt that some semblance of maturity began to arrive at last. I saved that final report card because it was the only one that seemed to justify those long years of agony.

While I was a senior, my very fine teacher of illustration, Miss Minette Paro, invited me to draw a series of cartoons about some of the activities around school for our senior annual. I was delighted to do this and set about it quickly, and promptly presented the drawings to Miss Paro. She seemed pleased with them, and I looked forward to the publishing of our yearbook, where I expected finally to see my cartoons on the printed page. The last day of school arrived and I thumbed anxiously through the annual, but found none of my drawings. To this day, I do not know why they were rejected. I have enjoyed a certain revenge, however, for ever since Peanuts was created I have received a steady stream of requests from high schools around the country to use the characters in their yearbooks. Eventually I accumulated a stack tall enough to reach the ceiling.

I think it is important for adults to consider what they were doing and what their attitudes were when they were the age their own children are now. There is no other real way of understanding the problems of children.

Charlie Brown's father is a barber, which is autobiographical, for our family's life revolved around the long hours my dad spent in his barbershop. He loved his work very much. I recall him telling me once that he really enjoyed getting up in the morning and going off to work. He was always in the barbershop by 8:00 in the morning, and during the 1930s he always worked until at least 6:30, and on Friday and Saturday nights, many times, until 8:00 or 9:00. He had one day off each week, Sunday, and his favorite sport was fishing. Occasionally, he would take my mother and me to a night baseball game or a hockey game, but fishing was always his main interest. It must have been disappointing to have a son who preferred golf.

Frequently in the evenings I went to the barbershop to wait for him to finish work and then walk home with him. He loved to read the comic strips, and we discussed them together and worried about what was going to happen next to certain of the characters. On Saturday evening, I would run up to the local drugstore at 9:00 when then Sunday pages were delivered and buy the two Minneapolis papers. The next morning, the two St. Paul papers would be delivered, so we had four comic sections to read. Several years later, when I became a delivery boy for one of the local printing firms, I used to pass the windows of the St. Paul *Pioneer Press* and look in where I could see the huge presses and the Sunday funnies tumbling down across the rollers. I wondered if I would ever see my own comics on those presses.

My mother also encouraged me in my drawing but, sadly, never lived to see any of my work published. She died a long, lingering death from cancer, when I was twenty, and it was a loss from which I sometimes believe I never recovered. Today it is a source of astonishment to me that I am older than she was when she died, and realizing this saddens me even more.

When I was thirteen, we were given a black-and-white dog who turned out to be the forerunner of Snoopy. He was a mixed breed and slightly larger than the beagle Snoopy is supposed to be. He probably had a little pointer in him and some other kind of hound, but he was a wild creature; I don't believe he was ever completely tamed. He had a "vocabulary" of understanding of approximately fifty words, and he loved to ride in the car. He waited all day for my dad to come home from the barbershop, and on Saturday evenings, just before 9:00, he always put his paws on my dad's chair to let him know it was time to get in the car and make the short drive up to the store to buy those newspapers. When I decided to put the dog in *Peanuts*, I used the general appearance of Spike, with similar markings. I had decided that the dog in the strip was to be named Sniffy, until one day, just before the strip was actually to be published, I was walking past a newsstand and glanced down at the rows of comic magazines. There I saw one about a dog named Sniffy, so I had to go back to my room and think of another name. Fortunately, before I even got home, I recalled my mother once saying that if we ever had another dog, we should name him Snoopy.

Not long ago I was looking through *The Art of Walt Disney*, a beautiful book, and there was a list of names that had been considered for The Seven Dwarfs. Lo and behold, one of the names that had been considered, but turned down, was Snoopy.

In my childhood, sports played a reasonably strong role, although they were strictly the sandlot variety. There was no organized Little League for us, even though we were all quite fanatical about baseball. Living in Minnesota restricted much of our sports activity, for the warmer seasons were short and clearly defined. Spring meant the coming of the marble season, and I loved playing marbles. When the baseball season came, we organized our own team and challenged those of other neighborhoods. We rarely had good fields for our games, and it was always our dream to play on a smooth infield and actually have a backstop behind the catcher so we wouldn't have to chase the foul balls. All too often, we would have to lift a manhole cover and lower someone to retrieve a baseball that had rolled along the curb and down into the sewer. We played a little tackle football, but more often touch football, as it was clearly less rough and did not have to be played on soft ground. In Minnesota, almost everyone knows how to skate, but I didn't actually learn on a real skating rink. Every sidewalk in front of every school had a sheet of ice at least ten feet long worn smooth from the kids sliding on it. It was on such a patch of ice, no longer than ten feet or wider than three feet, that I learned to skate. To play hockey on a real rink was a hopeless dream. Our hockey was usually played on a very tiny rink in one of our backyards, or in the street where we simply ran around with shoes rather than skates. The goals were two large clumps of snow, which were easily destroyed by inconsiderate drivers. I had always wanted to play golf, and had seen a series of Bobby Jones movie shorts when I was nine years old. There was no one to show me the game, and it was not until I was fifteen that I had a chance to try it. Immediately I fell totally in love with golf. I could think of almost nothing else for the next few years. I still wanted to be a cartoonist, but I also dreamed of becoming a great amateur golfer. Unfortunately, I never won anything except the caddy championship of Highland Park.

There are certain seasons in our lives that each of us can recall, and there are others that disappear from our memories like the melting snow. When I was fourteen, I had a summer that I shall always remember. We had organized our own neighborhood baseball team, but we never played on a strict schedule, for we didn't know when we could find another team to play. I lived about a block from a grade school called Maddocks in St. Paul where there was a rather large crushed-rock playground, which did have two baseball backstops, but no fences. A hard-hit ground ball could elude the second baseman or shortstop and very easily roll into the outfield so fast that none of the outfielders would be able to stop it, and it would be quite possible for a fast runner to beat it out for a home run. This field could also make sliding into second base reasonably painful if you were not careful. Fortunately, it was smooth enough so ground balls hit to the infielders did not take too many bad bounces.

A man named Harry (I never knew his last name) was the playground director that summer. He saw our interest in playing baseball and came up with the idea that we should organize four teams and have a summer league. This was the most exciting news that had come to any of us in a long time. There were two games each Tuesday and Thursday and I could hardly wait for them to begin. One game was to start at 9:00 between two of the teams, and the other game was to start at 10:30 between the other two teams. I was always at the field by 7:30 with all of my equipment, waiting for something to happen. Our team came in first place that year, probably because we practiced more than the other teams, and one day I actually pitched a no-hit, no-run game. It was a great summer and I wish that there was some way I could let that man, whom we knew only as Harry, know how much I appreciated it.

We knew little about Harry because boys that age are never quite that interested in people older than they. At my mother's suggestion, all the boys on our team chipped in and brought him a cake one day to demonstrate our appreciation for what he had done for us. He was a gentle man, probably not more than twenty-three or twenty-four, and I doubt if he was married. This was probably only a temporary job for him during times when it was difficult to find work, but he did his job well and he gave all of us a happy summer.

I have always tried to dig beneath the surface in my sports cartoons by drawing upon an intimate knowledge of the games. The challenges to be faced in sports work marvelously as a caricature of the challenges that we face in the more serious aspects of our lives. Anytime I experienced a crushing defeat in bowling, or had a bad night at bridge, or failed to qualify in the opening round of a golf tournament, I was able to transfer my frustrations to poor Charlie Brown. And when Charlie Brown has tried to analyze his own difficulties in life, he has always been able to express them best in sports terms.

During my senior year in high school, my mother showed me an ad that read: "Do you like to draw? Send in for our free talent test." This was my introduction to Art Instruction Schools, Inc., the correspondence school known at that time as Federal Schools. It was and still is located in Minneapolis, and even though, after signing up for the course, I could have taken my drawing there in person, I did all of the lessons by mail, as I would have had I lived several states away, for I was not that proud of my work.

I could have gone to one of several resident schools in the Twin Cities, but it was this correspondence course's emphasis upon cartooning that won me. The entire course came to approximately $170, and I remember my father having difficulty keeping up with the payments. I recall being quite worried when he received dunning letters, and when I expressed these worries to him he said not to become too concerned. I realized then that during those later Depression days he had become accustomed to owing people money. I eventually completed the course, and he eventually paid for it.

The two years following high school were extremely difficult, for this was the time that my mother was suffering so much with her illness. I was drafted during the month of February, in 1943, and spent several weeks at the induction center at Fort Snelling, Minnesota. We were allowed to go home on the weekends, and I recall how one Sunday evening, just before I had to return to Fort Snelling across the river from St. Paul, I went into the bedroom to say goodbye to my mother. She was lying in bed, very ill, and she said to me, "Yes, I suppose we should say good-bye because we probably will never see each other again." She died the next day and our tiny family was torn apart. I was shipped down to Camp Campbell, Kentucky, and my dad was left to try to put his life back together. He continued to work daily in the barbershop and finally accumulated a total of forty-five years working in the same place.

All of the summer-camp ideas that I have drawn are a result of my having absolutely no desire as a child to be sent away to a summer camp. To me, that was the equivalent to being drafted. When World War II came along, I met it with the same lack of enthusiasm. The three years I spent in the army taught me all I needed to know about loneliness, and my sympathy for the loneliness that all of us experience is dropped heavily upon poor Charlie Brown. I know what it is to have to spend days, evenings, and weekend by myself, and I also know how uncomfortable anxiety can be. I worry about almost all there is in life to worry about, and because I worry, Charlie Brown has to worry. I suppose our anxieties increase as we become responsible for more people. Perhaps some form of maturity should take care of this, but in my case it didn't. At any rate, I place the source of many of my problems on those three years in the army. The lack of any timetable or any idea as to when any of us would get out was almost unbearable. We used to sit around in the evenings and talk about things like this, and we were completely convinced that we were going to be in for the rest of our lives. The war seemed to have no end in sight. Yet, in spite of this, I recall a particular evening when I was on guard duty at the motor pool at the far end of the camp that is now called Fort Campbell, in the southern part of Kentucky; it was a beautiful summer evening, there was no one around in this area of the camp, and it was my job simply to see that no one interfered with any of the vehicles in that part of the motor pool, or tried to take any of them out of that particular gate. The only person in the world I had to worry about was my father, and I knew that he could take care of himself. As I sat there in the tiny guard shack, I seemed to be at complete peace with the world. Still, I knew for sure that I did not want to be where I was.

My mind has gone back to that hour many times, and I have tried to analyze why I should have been so at peace at that time. This is the kind of examination that produces some of the pages in

Peanuts, but of course it is covered up by little cartoon characters, using dialogue that is at once condensed and exaggerated. Why does the cartoonist see something funny in all of these anxieties? Is it because the cartoonist is afraid of complete commitment? Perhaps this is why so many draw about political or social problems rather than try to run for political office or participate in social work. Perhaps it demonstrates a certain character trait, as with the person who makes what starts out to be a serious statement, but then, realizing what he has said, qualifies it or steps back slightly, adding a self-conscious chuckle.

When I was just out of high school, I started to submit cartoons to most of the major magazines, as all the ambitious amateurs do, but received only the ordinary rejection slips and no encouragement. After World War II, however, I set about in earnest to sell my work. I visited several places in the Twin Cities to try to get some job in whatever art department might be able to use my limited talents, but I was unsuccessful. I was almost hired one day to letter tombstones and was glad when the man did not call me back the next day, for I had already begun to worry what my friends might say when I told them about my new job. One day, however, with my collection of sample comic strips in hand, I visited the offices of Timeless Topix, the publishers of a series of Catholic comic magazines. The art director, Roman Baltes, seemed to like my lettering and said, "I think I may have something for you to do." He gave me several comic-book pages that had already been drawn by others but with the balloons left blank, and he told me that I should fill in the dialogue. This was my first job, but soon after I took it I was also hired by Art Instruction. For the next year, I lettered comic pages for Timeless Topix, working sometimes until past midnight, getting up early the next morning, taking a streetcar to downtown St. Paul, leaving the work outside the door of Mr. Baltes' office, and then going over to Minneapolis to work at the correspondence school.

My job there was to correct some of the basic lessons, and it introduced me to a roomful of people who did much to affect my later life. The instructors at this correspondence school were bright, and the atmosphere in the large room was invigorating. Each person there seemed to have a special interest in some phase of commercial art or cartooning, and some even painting. The head of the department was Walter J. Wilwerding, a famous magazine illustrator of that period. Directly in front of me sat a man named Frank Wing who had drawn a special feature called "Yesterdays," which ran for a short time during the 1930s. He was a perfectionist at drawing things as they appeared, and I believe he did much to inspire me. He taught me the importance of drawing accurately, and even though I felt he was somewhat disappointed in me—and disapproved of my eventual drawing style—there is no doubt that I learned much from him. Almost nothing I draw now, in what is sometimes a quite extreme style, is not based on a real knowledge of how to draw that object, whether it be a shoe, a doghouse, or a child's hand. Cartooning, after all, is simply good design. In learning how to design a human hand after knowing how to draw it properly, one produces a good cartoon.

Some of the people who worked at Art Instruction Schools with me have remained friends all of these years, and I have used the names of several in the strip. Charlie Brown was named after my very good friend, Charlie Brown, whose desk was across the room. I recall perfectly the day he came over and first looked at the little cartoon face that had been named after him. "Is that what he looks like?" he expressed with dismay. The characters of Linus and Frieda were also named after friends of mine who were instructors.

Those were days filled with hilarity, for there was always some-one with a good joke, or laughter from some innocent mistake made by one of the students. It was not unusual for us to receive drawings of thumbs, and whenever we pulled such a drawing from its enve-lope we realized once again a student had misunderstood the expres-sion "making a thumbnail sketch." Another confusion came over the instruction to "experiment with matchstick figures"; students would actually send paper matchsticks glued to a sheet of paper.

There were many of us on the staff of Art Instruction who had ambitions to go on to other things, and I used my spare time, after completing the regular lesson criticisms, to work on my own car-toons. I tried never to let a week go by without having something in the mail working for me. During one period of time, from 1948 to 1950, I submitted cartoons regularly to the *Saturday Evening Post*, and sold fifteen of them. I was never able to break into any of the other magazines.

These were strongly formative years, and my ability to think of ideas and to present them properly was improving steadily. It seemed that it would be only a matter of time before I would be able to sell some type of marketable feature to a syndicate. I am still con-vinced that my eventual success was due largely to what I have called "the invigorating atmosphere" in the department of instruction at the correspondence school. I suppose it would be similar to that of a newspaper office. I had always dreamed of someday having a desk in a newspaper office, but it never came about.

It was an exciting time for me because I was involved in the very sort of thing I wished to do. I not only lettered the complete Timeless Topix in English, but would do the French and Spanish translations without having any idea as to what the balloons were saying. One day Roman bought a page of little panel cartoons that I had drawn and titled "Just Keep Laughing." One of the cartoons showed a small boy who looked prophetically like Schroeder sitting on the curb with a baseball bat in his hands talking to a little girl who looked pro-phetically like Patty. He was saying, "I think I could learn to love you,

Judy, if your batting average was a little higher." Frank Wing, my fellow instructor at Art Instruction, said, "Sparky, I think you should draw more of those little kids. They are pretty good." So I concentrated on creating a group of samples and eventually sold them as a weekly feature called *Li'l Folks* to the St. Paul *Pioneer Press*.

I was making regular trips to Chicago to try to sell a comic feature and was always gratified to talk with Mr. John Dille, Jr., at his National Newspaper Syndicate, for he was invariably kind and patient with me. This was not always true at some of the other syndicates. I dropped into the Chicago *Sun* one day and showed my work to Walt Ditzen, who was then their comic editor, and he was very impressed with what he saw. I recall him exclaiming, "I certainly cannot say no to this. We'll have to take it in to the president." We went into the man's office; he barely looked at the work and abruptly said, "No."

At this time I was also becoming a little more gregarious and was learning how to talk with people. When I first used to board the morning Zephyr and ride it to Chicago, I would make the entire trip without talking to anyone. Little by little, however, I was getting rid of my shyness and feelings of inferiority, and learning how to strike up acquaintances on the train and talk to people. Two conversations in the dining car remain with me. I was seated across from a nicely, but conservatively, dressed gentleman one time on my way to Chicago; we introduced ourselves, and he asked me about the nature of my trip. After I had explained a little about myself, he told me that he was a Methodist minister, to which I replied, "Yes, I sort of figured you were a minister." As I was saying this I knew, as we all too frequently do in such situations, that I was saying the wrong thing, but it came out before I could stop myself. Then, of course, I had to explain why I had deduced that he was a minister without offending him, even though the conclusion could be just as flattering as insulting. On my return trip to St. Paul, I struck up a conversation with another extremely interesting man who turned out to be the publisher of a small music magazine. Because I was just beginning to become acquainted with classical music, and because I was so interested in the entire subject, yet so clearly a layman, I had much to ask him. I had recently purchased Berlioz's *Harold in Italy*, and had fallen in love with its many melodic passages. I asked him what he thought of *Harold in Italy*. He considered this for several moments before looking at me and saying, "Well, the human ear is a strange thing." I didn't dare ask him what he meant. I had the feeling it would be better not to know.

I continued to mail my work out to major syndicates. One day I opened up a letter from one syndicate that turned me down, and then opened another letter from the director of NEA in Cleveland saying he liked my work very much. Arrangements were made during the next few months for me to start drawing a Sunday feature for NEA, but at the last minute their editors changed their minds and I had to start all over. In the spring of 1950 I accumulated a batch of some of the better cartoons I had been drawing for the St. Paul paper and mailed them off to United Feature Syndicate in New York. I don't know how much time went by without my hearing from them, but I'm sure it was at least six weeks. Convinced that my drawings had been lost in the mail, I finally wrote them a letter, describing the drawings I had sent and asking them if they could recall receiving anything similar. If not, I wanted to know so that I could put a tracer on the lost cartoons. Instead, I received a very nice letter from Jim Freeman, their editorial director, who said they were very interested in my work and would I care to come to New York and talk about it.

That was an exciting trip. When I arrived at the Syndicate offices early in the morning, no one other than the receptionist was there. I had brought along a new comic strip I had been working on, rather than the panel cartoons that United Feature had seen. I simply wanted to give them a better view of my work. I told the receptionist that I had not had breakfast yet, so I would go out and eat and then return. When I got back to the Syndicate offices, they had already decided they would rather publish the strip than the panel. This made me very happy, for I preferred the strip myself. I returned to

Minneapolis filled with great hope for the future and asked a certain girl to marry me. When she turned me down and married someone else, there was no doubt that Charlie Brown was on his way. Losers get started early.

Charles M. Schulz, *Peanuts Jubilee: My Life and Art with Charlie Brown and Others* (New York: Holt, Rinehart and Winston, 1975), 11-36.

Peanuts as Profession of Faith

An interviewer once wrote that one of my characters, Charlie Brown, mirrors some of my own childhood troubles. That may be true, but he is also a reflection of the troubles of millions of others—or so I gather from those who write me. I think Charlie is a reflection of something in all of us which needs constant reassuring that the people round about us really do like us.

Linus' affection for his blanket, on the other hand, is a symbol of the things we cling to. Our first three children, when they were small, all carried blankets around the house with them. But some of our *adult* habits are ridiculous. Not long ago I had Linus' blanket-hating grandmother come to his house for a visit. She tried to get him to give up his propensity for the blanket; so he threw up to her the fact that she was drinking 32 cups of coffee a day!

I grew up an only child, and my mother died the very week I was drafted. This was a tremendous blow to our little family. I was assigned to the 20th Armored Division and eventually became a machine gun squad leader. Our division was shipped to Germany just before the war ended, and we took part in the liberation of Dachau and Munich. We were also assigned to the proposed invasion of Japan which never materialized.

Before going into the armed forces I met a minister from a local congregation. He walked into my father's barbershop one day in St.

Paul, Minnesota, and we became friends. It was not long after that that we called him to preach my mother's funeral sermon. After coming back from the Army, I began to attend services at his church. We had an active group of young people—all of us were in our twenties—and we began studying the Bible together.

The more I thought about the matter during those studying times, the more I realized that I really loved God. I recognized the fact that He had pulled me through a depression in which I had been torn apart from everything I knew, and that He had enabled me to survive so many experiences. These realizations did not come upon me at any particular great moment of decision. I never went forward at a Sunday evening service. I cannot point to a specific time of dedication to Christ. I was just suddenly "there," and did not know when it happened that I arrived.

I accepted Jesus Christ by gratitude. I have always been grateful for the things the Lord has provided me with: good health, education, family, and the experiences of World War II which have now passed into history.

Since those youth group days, we have all moved to different areas, and many of us have become active in other churches. I teach the adult Sunday School class in a church in Sebastopol, California. I am trying to encourage the new members in particular to raise questions and to present their views in class without fear or embarrassment. It is terrible, of course, to be a beginner in anything and to feel that you don't know enough about the subject. Most people feel that way about the Bible. The idea is to create a climate in which people will not be afraid to ask even little questions. And it is such a thrill when you find someone saying that he is doing some outside reading and that for the first time in his life he is studying the Bible on his own.

In my cartooning I draw for two kinds of editors: secular editors and church editors. I work for the secular press through a newspaper syndicate, and naturally I must exercise care in the way I go about expressing things. I have a message that I want to present,

LOOK AT THE BUMP ON THE BACK OF MY HAND..

YOU HAVE A "GANGLION"

YOU KNOW HOW THEY SAY TO CURE IT? YOU HAVE SOMEONE HIT IT WITH A BIBLE!

WITH A WHAT?

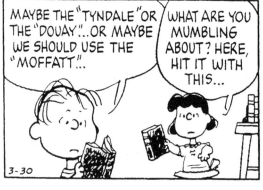

MAYBE THE "TYNDALE" OR THE "DOUAY"...OR MAYBE WE SHOULD USE THE "MOFFATT"...

WHAT ARE YOU MUMBLING ABOUT? HERE, HIT IT WITH THIS...

BONK!

3-30

but I would rather bend a little to put over a point than to have the whole strip dropped because it is too obvious. As a result, all kinds of people in religious work have written to thank me for preaching in my own way through the strips. That is one of the things that keeps me going.

Sometimes people ask whether our children (they range in age from six to fourteen years) supply me with most of my ideas. For the most part I have to say that they do not; nor do I get many ideas from watching pets. Snoopy, you see, is more a result of reflection than of observation. You just don't see dogs lying around on top of doghouses!

As I said, I also work for church magazine editors, and my teen-age cartoons appear in about seventy different church publications every week. This is a different medium. I step out now and then and say a few things which people don't want to see in cartoons. But I am trying to teach some of the church publication editors that if you do not say anything in a cartoon, you might as well not draw at all. Humor which does not say anything is worthless.

So I contend that a cartoonist must be given a chance to do his own preaching. I say to the editors, "You have to give us room to work, and you have to tolerate us, too, and not regard the cartoon as a mere 'filler.'" Of course, I am very fond of my editor friends and am surprised and happy that such a variety of groups is publishing this work.

This comes back to my relationship of gratitude. I feel a constant gratefulness to God for His patience with me and with all of us. I cannot fail to be thrilled every time I read the things that Jesus said, and I am more and more convinced of the necessity of following Him. What Jesus means to me is this: in Him we are able to see God and to understand His feelings toward us.

I am still a believer in what the church refers to as "holy living." I think it is applicable for a person in whatever profession he may be working. We were able to prove a good point in the publishing of *Happiness Is a Warm Puppy* a couple of years ago. One needs only to look quickly around him to see the great quantity of useless literature being published, and yet there was a market for a book which was absolutely pure in content to the extent that it immediately sold a million copies. What does this mean to those who cry that the public wants things which are only low and degrading? I think each of us who deals in any way with things which are creative and things which are going to be read or looked at or heard by the public, needs always to test himself by the eighth verse in the fourth chapter of the book of Philippians: "Finally, brethren, whatsoever things are just, whatsoever things are pure, whatsoever things are lovely, whatsoever things are of good report; if there be any virtue, and if there be any praise, think on these things."

Recently I published a little series of cartoons on the subject of security. Perhaps the way I feel about Christ is best told in the last cartoon of that series. Linus is kneeling with his arms on his bed, and the caption reads, "Security is knowing you are not alone."

Charles M. Schulz, "Peanuts," *Collegiate Challenge*, 1963.

Commencement Address at Saint Mary's College

I would like to use a text from Romans 8:26 as a basis for my thought this morning. "Likewise the Spirit helps us in our weakness; for we do not know how to pray as we ought, but the Spirit himself intercedes for us with sighs too deep for words."

Saint Mary's College is to be complimented for its courage. It is probably the only college in the country which has invited a comic strip artist to be its Commencement Day speaker. I take this as not only a great personal compliment, but also a great compliment to a profession that is not always treated so well. There is great tendency to downgrade some of the professions that make up the list of what we sometimes call the lively arts, and the comic strip is usually placed at the very bottom of that list. In spite of this, about ninety million people read the funnies every day, and take them quite seriously.

I must admit that I am always amazed at the public response to some of the episodes in *Peanuts*. During the past few months I have been receiving letters from people who have either fought the Red Baron in Sopwith Camels or are very familiar with the areas around the front lines where Snoopy always gets shot down. A few weeks ago I received calls from people around the country begging to have Linus and Lucy move back into the neighborhood. I told them that I had no control over the company that was transferring Linus' and Lucy's father to a new city. One Sunday morning, however, we stirred up some trouble that I absolutely never anticipated. In the paper that came out that morning Charlie Brown and all his friends were playing croquet. Lucy had just hit Charlie Brown's ball, and had driven it a couple of blocks down the street. In fact, she had hit it so far that the last panel showed Charlie Brown standing in an outdoor telephone booth. He was saying, "Call me when it's my turn. The number is 343-2794."

Now, when I thought of drawing this page, I had intended to put in my own telephone number. However, I thought of a better idea. I have a very close friend who lives in Burlingame. He is the producer of our animated television shows, and he loves to talk to people on the phone. This was a natural! Why not put his number in the comic strip? Well, on that fateful Sunday morning the telephone rang the first time at six o'clock. It continued to ring steadily until past nine o'clock that evening, and each time it was answered, voices of different ages would say, "It's your turn, Charlie Brown."

Another Sunday page that stirred up considerable interest is appropriate today because it has to do with visions, hopes, and dreams. Charlie Brown, Lucy, and Linus are lying on top of a small knoll looking up at some puffy clouds floating across the sky, and Lucy says, "If you use your imagination, you can see lots of things in the cloud formations . . . What do you think you see, Linus?"

"Well, those clouds up there look to me like the map of the British Honduras on the Caribbean . . . That cloud up there looks a little like the profile of Thomas Eakins, the famous painter and sculptor . . . And that group of clouds over there gives me the impression of the stoning of Saint Stephen . . . I can see the Apostle Paul standing there to one side . . ."

"That's very good," says Lucy. "What do you see in the clouds, Charlie Brown?"

"Well, I was going to say I saw a ducky and a horsie, but I've changed my mind!"

During this past week, speakers on campuses all across the country have been talking to graduates about many subjects. When

we did the Christmas show for television last year, we wanted to do something that would show the children's search for the true meaning of Christmas, and after days of pondering, I finally decided that every idea we had was an idea that really avoided the essential truth which was that the true meaning of Christmas could be found only in the Gospel according to Saint Luke and so we had Linus recite those famous passages. The same thing is happening here today. No matter what I consider to say, I come back to a passage in the New Testament that contains a truth in which I firmly believe. In the last chapter of the Book of John we find Peter and Thomas, Nathaniel, the sons of Zebedee, and two others who are unnamed turning back to their old profession of fishing. Now, it is possible to read these stories many times before certain truths filter through to us. I recall reading the dramatic conflict between the devil and Jesus on the mountaintop. The devil had offered to Jesus all the kingdoms of this world, and Jesus turned him down. We read this story and we think only of the fact that Jesus turned down the opportunity to be a ruler of Israel. But Jesus recognized something that many of us take years to realize. The truth of the confrontation was that the devil was lying! The devil did not have the power to give all the kingdoms of the world to Jesus. If Jesus had yielded to the temptation, He would have been destroyed immediately by Roman authorities.

And so as we move over the shore of the Sea of Tiberius we find Peter and his friends returning at dawn from fishing. A figure is standing on shore by a small charcoal fire. They gather round this fire, none daring to speak even though they know it is Jesus who has been waiting for them. Jesus turns to Peter, and asks, "Simon, son of John, do you love me more than these?" "Yes, Lord, You know that I love you." Jesus said to him, "Feed my Lambs." Then a second time Jesus asks, "Simon, son of John, do you love me?" and Peter answers, "Yes, Lord, You know that I love you." Jesus said, "Tend my sheep." Then a third time Jesus turns to Peter, and asks, "Simon, son of John, do you love me?" Imagine the flood of words that could have sprung from Peter's mouth at this time. The explanations, the apologies, the tears of anguish, but Peter has a better answer. It is the answer of supreme faith. "Lord, you know everything; You know that I love you."

When the excitement of these days passes away, and when some of the visions begin to grow a little dim; when it becomes impossible to put into words the prayer you want to speak, then we must be able to lift our heads up, and say with all faith as Peter did, "Lord, you know that I love you."

Delivered June 11, 1966.

Charles Schulz
and *Peanuts*

In all the articles that have been written about Charlie Brown
and Snoopy and the other things we have been doing, none of
the writers has ever mentioned that the one cartoonist who
helped most was Walt Ditzen. When he was working for one of the
syndicates in Chicago, I dropped in with a batch of samples and he
went far out of his way that day and later to give me advice and help
that I badly needed. I have always regretted that Walt never got any
credit for this where people could hear about it.

Peanuts started as a space-saving comic strip, and although I am
sure this helped to sell it and keep it in some of the papers that otherwise might not have given it room, I have always felt guilty about it
because I am sure it helped to start a dangerous trend. It is a pity that
we somehow cannot cooperate in spite of the tremendous rivalries
that exist and produce syndicated material that would be of a standard
size. I learned a long time ago that I was going to have to struggle for
attention on the comic page when I had the smallest amount of space
and others were using black borders and all sorts of dramatic heavy
areas to gain attention. One of the best ways, of course, to counteract
this was simply to use a little more white space.

Jud [Hurd] has asked me to talk about whatever happens to
come to mind, so a couple of other things have occurred to me that
are related to the whole problem of trying to maintain our profession

in a time when some people seem to think it is struggling for exis-
tence. I am not that pessimistic about our medium, but I do think
there are many areas that need improving. I think one of the worst
things is the system of trying to please readers who subscribe to
only the daily or only the Sunday feature. By duplicating Saturday,
Sunday, and Monday you punish the reader who follows the strip
all the way through. I know that syndicates vary in their approach
on this, but I think it is a foolish system; there is enough flexibil-
ity in our medium either to run separate stories or not to worry so
much about the continuity. I also am convinced that there should be
a lot less crime in comic strips. Mystery stories are wonderful and
adventure is an absolute necessity, but anything that follows television trends is fatal. In fact, the moment a cartoonist forgets that he
is dealing in a different medium and tries instead to duplicate the
movie or television screen, he is on the wrong track.

For those of you who may be interested, I have now moved my
studio to the Redwood Empire Ice Arena, which my wife and I built
three years ago and where Warren Lockhart also has his office. Warren and I have formed a new corporation called Creative Develop-
ments, and out of this have come many new ideas for television programs and a very close working relationship with various licensees
who handle our side products. Our major project at the moment is
the new movie we are doing with Lee Mendelson and Bill Melendez.
It is to be called *Snoopy Come Home*, and I think it will be ten times
better than the last movie we made, *A Boy Named Charlie Brown*. We
have learned a good deal since we made that one, and we have high
hopes that people will really like this new feature. My role is that
of writer. I have complete editorial control of the movie and have
written all the dialogue and have created every bit of business that
you will see on the screen. Fortunately, working with Lee and Bill is
very easy, for each of us never encroaches upon the other's area of
responsibility. I know what I want in the movie, but I also know my
limitations and am perfectly willing to allow the animators to use
their imagination where it is demanded for certain scenes.

Something just occurred to me. Due to a misunderstanding in a discussion about my background while riding in an elevator with Carl Rose, I have either been given credit or have been blamed for being a Protestant minister. Sometimes I am referred to as an ex-minister of the Methodist church or a Presbyterian, but actually I have never been anything of the sort. I am strictly a lay theologian and have never pretended to be more than that. The two books that Robert Short wrote were of his own doing and contained ideas and views that were strictly his. I will admit, however, that I have used many scriptural references in *Peanuts* and have always enjoyed doing this. It has opened up a whole new area of thought and has brought in readers from almost every religious denomination, although it has also brought in criticism from those who feel that the Bible should not be quoted in what they call "something as lowly as a comic strip."

I think the *Peanuts* strip itself has changed considerably during the past five years. I am probably using fewer gags than ever before and am depending on the personalities of the characters to carry the strip. I have learned also to trust the faithfulness of my readers, and I certainly never expect to please each one every day. I have learned to take the risk of using ideas that might be regarded as too "in," knowing that those who understand the idea will be flattered and will appreciate it by showing even more attention to the strip than they did before. Probably the most "in" idea I have ever used was the one where Snoopy was pulling the sled up the hill and when Charlie Brown looked down at the sled, he saw that it was named Rosebud. I also love to do things that are really kind of silly, like using terms such as *queensnakes* and *gully cats* but realize that this is very risky because if readers are caught in a mood where they do not appreciate silliness and do not see it in this way, the whole thing is going to collapse, but I am convinced that these risks are worth taking, and I am fortunate in having editors at United Feature Syndicate who are willing to go along with this kind of thing.

The Christmas That Almost Got Stolen

I t is probably impossible to discuss holidays and children without talking about school. No matter how much meaning we try to put into holiday ceremonies, children will always look to these times primarily as a reprieve from schoolwork.

When I recall my childhood in St. Paul, Minnesota, the memories invariably are memories of school. I was not overfond of the class routines, but I must admit there was always one project that I enjoyed. Just as English class meant the inevitable theme "What I Did on My Summer Vacation," art class always included a project requiring us to draw our friends engaged in some form of winter activity. Now, in Minnesota this meant that we drew a group of children skating on a pond. This did *not* mean that any of us had actually experienced such an activity; we were city kids, and very few of us had ever seen a pond that had frozen hard enough to be skated on. But we always tried to depict these scenes, and it was a certainty that every child included a hole in the ice out of which projected a sign that read "Danger." Most likely we had seen these in comic strips.

I noticed that all the kids had trouble drawing those holes in the ice. Somehow they just looked like black spots. My own interest in cartooning led me to discover that by drawing a double line in the ice, one could depict the thickness of that ice. I was very proud when the teacher came around and complimented me on my discovery.

This was one of my very few moments of triumph in school. Unfortunately, the memory of a Minnesota Christmas that always comes back to me has to do with another, less-successful project.

At the beginning of each December I looked forward to the holidays as happily as any child. I loved the decorations in the downtown shopping areas and I eagerly anticipated the gifts I might receive. But the best part of the holiday was the knowledge that we would have a two-week vacation from school—and how I looked forward to that! Inevitably, however, there always seemed to be one teacher who could not resist darkening the vacation days with a homework assignment, and one particular vacation was spoiled by our having to read *Silas Marner*. Why couldn't this be read during the regular school term? Why couldn't we be allowed to relax for 14 days and read our comic books and our magazines about football and hockey heroes? *Silas Marner* was pure drudgery.

Now, of course, we all know that 14 days, even to a teen-ager, is close to an eternity. There would be no reason at all to begin reading a novel during the first few days of vacation, for wouldn't the vacation stretch on forever? And then, of course, as the first week disappeared, why would you want to begin reading the novel during the first part of the second week? After all, you had still had seven full days. And then as those days disappeared, one by one, and you drew near the end of the second week, there was still no reason to panic— you had the whole weekend, and anyone who could read reasonably fast could surely read *Silas Marner* over the weekend. So, of course, there was nothing to worry about.

But weekends go very fast, and before you know it, Sunday night has arrived. The book has not been opened and there is no possible way to finish reading it in one evening. The only thing left is to dread Monday morning.

Why do teachers have to give such assignments? Why can't we read books that are more interesting? Why are teachers so unreasonable? Why do we have to go to school anyway? Why do Christmas vacations go by so fast? Why are Monday mornings the worst kind of morning ever created?

Oh, how I hated to return to school that day! When was I ever going to learn? The next time we got an assignment like this, I would know better, but it was too late now. I was on my way to school and I was on my way to certain doom.

When I walked into English class that Monday morning there was a strange excitement in the room. Our teacher had not shown up yet and no one knew why. Then we were given the news. During Christmas vacation she had slipped and fallen on the ice and had broken her arm. Off the hook! We were off the hook! Our assignment was canceled and we would not have to finish *Silas Marner* until our teacher returned to school.

This may not be the kind of memory adults like to think children have about Christmas holidays, but I am afraid this is the kind they have.

Merry Christmas. If you have any homework, do it early, and be careful walking on the ice.

Charles M. Schulz, "The Christmas That Almost Got Stolen," *Redbook Magazine*, December, 1976, 92, 94.

Snoopy's Senior World Hockey Tournament

1935 was a good sports year for me. That summer I saw my first professional baseball game, and that winter I saw the St. Paul hockey team play Wichita in what was then the United States Hockey League. The hockey we played as kids in our neighborhood was on either a ridiculously small rink that my dad made for us in our backyard or else out in the snow-covered street. The goals were always two clumps of snow, which worked quite well until an inconsiderate woman driver crushed them as we all stood to the side yelling raucous remarks.

Our house had a typical Minnesota basement, and beneath the stairs there was an area that was just wide enough to simulate a hockey goal. I had a very accommodating 65-year-old grandmother who was willing to stand in the goal with a broom while I shot tennis balls at her. She really knew nothing about sports, but loved to follow the accomplishments of the local teams. Her favorite heroine, of course, was Patty Berg, even though she never understood golf scoring.

Many years later, my own family and I made our big move to northern California. For a long time, our only regret with this move was that we could no longer keep up our ice skating. Rumor had it that across town there was an arena, which we finally visited one night and eventually renewed our skating. Just as our two boys began to develop a few hockey skills, and our two youngest girls discovered

HERE'S THE WORLD FAMOUS HOCKEY PLAYER ON HIS WAY TO THE GAME..

UNDER T
IF YOU S
ARE AUTO.
FROM

1-27

OLES
HT, YOU
JECTED
...

SO I MIGHT AS WELL GO HOME NOW..

© 1983 United Feature Syndicate, Inc.

the excitement of show skating, the arena developed structural difficulties and had to close. I remember remarking to my wife, "I wish there were something we could do about it," and she answered, "I was hoping you would say that."

Two years later, the community saw the completion of what has been described as the world's most beautiful ice arena. It is dedicated to the public's enjoyment of skating. We have our serious skaters, of course, and we put on the most extravagant and beautiful ice shows that you can see anyplace. We even hold symphony concerts, and after covering the ice we hold an annual women's tennis tournament with such greats as Billie Jean King, Rosie Casals, and Virginia Wade.

What has become probably our most looked-forward-to event each July, however, is Snoopy's Senior World Hockey Tournament. I recall this past summer, standing by the rail with a man who formerly played in Czechoslovakia. He remarked, "I stood here for nine years waiting to be old enough to play in this tournament." Our minimum age bracket is 40, and we play in five-year brackets, going on up to what next year will be our first 65-year-old bracket. The men in that age group have been complaining that they are tired of "chasing those 60-year-old kids around."

Our gratitude toward the men who come all the way across our country and from Canada, or even from Finland and Japan, makes us try to put on the best tournament we can. We host an outdoor barbecue, and on Saturday night, before the Sunday finals, we have entertainment for the men and their wives, which includes a dance. The actual play during the tournament is typical of senior hockey, which means no body-checking or slap shots. Actually, we sometimes feel this produces a better brand of hockey, for the emphasis then turns toward fast skating and good passing plays. Our more fanatic spectators appreciate being able to see many of the former National Hockey League stars who have now entered senior life but still put on marvelous exhibitions of their talent.

Strange things do happen, of course. My team—and I use the expression humbly—was suiting up a couple of years ago when we heard that the goalie, who was in action in the game in progress, had just hurt his leg. His team had no substitute, but the goalie whose team we were preparing to play was suited up and ready to go. He went in as a substitute, but found himself in a much faster game than the one he was prepared for. His team was composed of men over 60, and he now found himself in a tie game of men in their 40s. He put on a superb performance, however, and shut out the opponents for the remainder of the third period and then the five-minute overtime. His new teammates pounded him on the back and congratulated him for his heroic goaltending. The next game he started against our team, which then went out and scored nine goals against him. This is what can happen in Snoopy's Senior World Hockey Tournament.

It takes the work of 50 to 100 dedicated volunteers to put on our tournament, but I believe the joy that we get seeing the excitement of the games makes it worthwhile, and I have said many times that these seniors deserve something in return for what they have put in toward youth hockey. Almost all of these men work as coaches or referees at arenas were they come from, and this helps to repay them for their dedication.

It is time now, of course, to begin planning for our 11th tournament, and I imagine we will all have at least 40 teams. Each year we wonder if we can surpass our last year's event, but somehow it happens.

Charles M. Schulz, "Snoopy's Senior World Hockey Tournament," *Christian Science Monitor*, November 28, 1984, 42.

I'll Be Back in Time for Lunch

Sometimes it takes me a long time to come to certain conclusions. I have been drawing the *Peanuts* strip for almost 35 years now and, of course, have had many strangers visit my studio. They look at all the books in my room and at a beautiful glass-top desk, given to me by my wife as a wedding present, upon which I place the strips after they have been drawn. They then look at my drawing board and express amazement that this is the *actual* board at which I sit and draw the strips. I often wonder whether they think that it is there merely as an exhibit and that the real board, some mysterious object, is hidden away in another room.

Inevitably, the conversation turns to how far ahead I work. When they learn about the six-week daily-strip deadline and the 12-week Sunday-page deadline, a visitor almost never fails to remark: "Gee, you could work real hard, couldn't you, and get several months ahead and then take the time off?"

Being, as I said, a slow learner, it took me until last year to realize what an odd statement that really is. You don't work all of your life to do something so you don't have to do it. I could talk about Beethoven knocking out a few fast symphonies so he could take some time off; or Picasso grinding out a dozen paintings so he could go away, but the comparison would obviously be pompous.

We live in a society that worships vacations. It seems that I have not learned the proper technique. I do remember, of course, how I looked forward to Christmas vacations when I was in school, and Army furloughs were something to be really cherished. Now, however, things have changed.

My father ran a barber shop in St. Paul, Minnesota, for 45 years, and I do not recall him ever taking a real vacation. Frequently, on Saturday nights after he closed the shop, he, my mother and I might drive to some lake in northern Minnesota for a weekend fishing trip. I was not much of a fisherman, but it was the one sport that he loved and that he and my mother could share. His excuse for these mini-vacations was that he could not afford to take off from work, and, during those Depression days, he was mostly right. As I look back, however, and put a few conclusions together, I have decided that he simply had a fear of travel.

Somehow, I think, that I have, perhaps, inherited the same fear. In spite of this, my wife and I and sometimes other friends have traveled to Europe, where we have watched the matches at Wimbledon and have toured the various sights around London and certain areas of France. A very emotional trip back to Normandy included visits to Omaha Beach and to a chateau near Rouen. I also enjoyed very much a trip down the Rhine from Basel, Switzerland, to Amsterdam, for I was anxious to see what the area around Remagen looked like. When our outfit crossed the river toward the end of World War II, it was dusk, and we had no idea of the appearance of the landscape. Thus, these vacations have included some marvelous highlights.

When I have felt uneasy while traveling, I have tried my hand at outdoor sketching. Although I never draw merely for the fun of it, I am always amazed at the joy and relaxation it can bring—even though most of the felt-pen sketches that I do on these trips never really amount to much.

This uneasiness at being away from home has been diagnosed as a fear of being out of control. Perhaps that is why some of the shorter vacations, such as simply going down to play in the annual Crosby Pro-Am, bring me such satisfaction. I have done it often and I am among friends, and there is a wonderful gratification in being invited.

PEANUTS

featuring

"Good ol' Charlie Brown"

by SCHULZ

SIGH

I NEED A VACATION, BUT IT'S HARD TO GET AWAY THESE DAYS.. THERE'S JUST SO MUCH TO DO...

I CAN'T KEEP GOING THE WAY I'VE BEEN, THOUGH... I HAVE TO GET AWAY.. I DESERVE A VACATION..

SUPPERTIME !

Several years ago, I drew a strip where Charlie Brown's little sister, Sally, said that she didn't mind going on any kind of a trip as long as she could be home by noon. I think I know how she feels.

When others tell me that they are going off on a two-week or two-month journey, I have a difficult time comprehending just what it is they are going to do for all that time. How do they actually get up in the morning without having any particular assignment? I think that I can learn to do this. I know I am trying. But then, there are always those daily strips and those Sunday pages that have to be drawn.

It is a problem, but I am working on it.

Charles M. Schulz, "I'll Be Back in Time for Lunch," *Los Angeles Times*, March 17, 1985, 16.

The Fan:
Baseball Is Life, I'm Afraid

By Charlie Brown

Baseball is life, I'm afraid. Well, I love baseball. I suppose I love it so much because I love standing on the mound where I can look over the whole game and field and feel I'm in control. What a beautiful feeling that is, wow!

I admit, however, I don't have much to be proud of. I have a dog at shortstop whose big fantasy is to play hockey, of all things, against Wayne Gretzky. I have this kid at second base who holds a security blanket. Then I have Lucy, who's probably the worst right fielder in the game. The only good thing she has are excuses. She either gets clouds in her eyes, or she says, "The grass got in my eyes." It's gotten to the point that I'm actually looking forward to what her next excuse will be.

Schroeder, of course, is my catcher. Things are so bad with my team that he doesn't even give me signals. He knows that the other teams don't care what I throw anyway.

None of this really matters, though. It doesn't even bother me that my team doesn't have a name, or that we use old motel pillows for bases.

The game of baseball, and me being a pitcher—those are the things that count. With me as the pitcher, and, of course, the manager, I call the shots over my life, and isn't that what all the people

want? Even though having control over my team is like having control over nothing, I still love the game—it has a beauty you don't find in other sports.

That's why my dream has always been that someday I'd be at a major league game, and someone would hit a foul ball and I'd make this spectacular, totally incredible catch. Then the manager of the home team would come out of the dugout and say, "Sign that kid up, fast." I was telling this to one of my friends, and you know what he said? Well, he told me, "Yeah, yeah. You and about 20 million other kids."

I'm a hero-worshipper, and there's so much about the game that's heroic—making diving catches in the field, leaping up against an outfield wall to make a game-saving catch, hitting a home run, or even striking out one of Peppermint Patty's kids from across town. Too bad all those things are just fantasies of mine. My team is so bad, we don't even have uniforms. And you know what Patty once told me? She said she could never marry anyone she could strike out in three straight pitches.

I'd like to be a strikeout king myself. I'd love to have a change of pace, but as it turns out, every pitch I throw is the same. Schroeder once walked out to the mound and said, "I like that slowball you just threw." He knows how to hurt a guy. I was throwing my fastest, fastest fastball.

The other thing that makes baseball great is you have an entire team to root for, you can pick your heroes from a whole group of guys. Baseball is a game that builds heroes—and also goats. So far I've only been a goat.

I think my best talent is avoiding those line drives that whiz by the mound. They could tear off my shoes, socks, hat, shorts, everything. The complaint is that it would take me too long to get dressed.

Don't' get me wrong, I look forward to playing. But the baseball season is hard on me. I don't sleep at night thinking about the next day's game. My sister Sally even asked me once if I was superstitious like other players. I said, yes. She said, "What difference does it make? You always lose anyway." That's the way little sisters are.

Unfortunately, in a way she's right. All winter I got ready for the season looking at our team's statistics—who got the hits, who drove in runs. It's surprising how fast I did this. We never get any hits. Errors is our big column.

What's great about baseball is that it can be enjoyed in Yankee Stadium or on a field near a picnic area. Baseball has all of these marvelous levels that truly make it the national pastime.

I like the fact that baseball doesn't have to be totally organized, that a group of people can grab their gloves, virtually anyplace, and have just as much fun, if not more, than in the games played at Dodger Stadium.

Baseball sort of reflects the problems we have in our lives— fear, loneliness, despair, losing—all these things can be talked about through the medium of baseball. That reminds me of what Linus once said to me: "Baseball is a caricature of life." I looked at him and said, "Gosh, that's a relief. I was afraid it was life."

Charlie Brown [Charles M. Schulz], "The Fan: Baseball is Life, I'm Afraid," *Inside Sports*, May, 1985, 82.

HERE'S THE WORLD WAR I FLYING ACE RETURNING TO THE AIRDROME IN HIS SOPWITH CAMEL..	AS USUAL, HE GOES TO THE SMALL FRENCH CAFE WHERE HE CAN FORGET HIS TROUBLES, THE WAR..EVERYTHING!	BON SOIR, MC ACE..WHAT

4-9

Comic Inspiration

I'm not often asked where I get my ideas for drawing *Peanuts*, like that little French café where Snoopy sits and passes the time talking to the waitress. I don't know exactly where that idea came from—drawing a comic strip is sort of a mysterious process—but I have been to Paris a few times over the years.

During my last visit, the Louvre put on a one-man show with the original artwork from about 80 *Peanuts* strips. The French gave me a nice medal, and I was awarded the title of Commander of Arts and Letters—not bad for a guy who just draws a dog and little kids with big heads.

As a celebration, my family and I had dinner at Maxim's. Even though I'd eaten there once before, the whole experience was something of a mystery: You're not quite sure what you're ordering, you don't know what anything costs, and everything is pompous. But

dining at Maxim's is one of those experiences everyone should have at least once.

I'd visited France long before that, during World War II, when my squad got off the troopship in February 1945 and was stationed briefly at a château near Rouen—the Château Malvoisin, which means the "house of the bad neighbor." I used to think and dream about that building all the time. It was gray stone, with a stone wall around it forming a paddock where my squad set up camp.

A few years ago I went back to see the château, and there I got the idea for the movie *Bon Voyage, Charlie Brown*, where Charlie Brown and his friends go to France as exchange students. Naturally, they spend a night at the château.

It's funny how images from your travels stick in your mind. The first trip I remember was when I was six. I grew up in St. Paul, Minnesota, where my dad had a barbershop. (Charlie Brown's dad is also a barber.) My father decided to move to Needles, California, so we piled into our 1928 Ford and drove across America.

We camped out every night; I used to wonder what it would be like to stay in a hotel. We either pitched a big tent in a campground or stopped overnight in what they called tourist cabins. Each one was just a box with nothing in it. It was the era when Americans first took to the highways to see the country. Along the road I remember standing on a picnic table and getting my first glimpse of the mountains far in the distance; I suppose they were the Rockies. I can still see them.

Finally we arrived in Needles on a very hot night—most nights in Needles are very hot—and we lived there for a year. In my comic strip, Snoopy's brother Spike lives near this same desert town, where we usually see him sitting by a saguaro. But I didn't get my idea of his surroundings from childhood memories. Mine is just a cartoon desert, a made-up place.

Most comic strip ideas are like that. They come from sitting in a room alone and drawing seven days a week, as I've done for 40 years. And some things from my travels would never fit into *Peanuts* anyway. I'll never forget a cruise my daughter and I took with three other couples to Puerto Vallarta, Mexico. When our ship docked, a friend and I went for a lunchtime stroll through the picturesque seaside town—and bumped into Elizabeth Taylor and Richard Burton. It's hard to believe, but they invited us up to their home and showed us around. I remember that the house was hung with paintings and had lots of open windows.

It was quite an experience. After all, is there a man on earth who wouldn't like to spend 20 minutes with Elizabeth Taylor? But I don't think we'll ever get to see it in *Peanuts*.

Charles M. Schulz, "Comic Inspiration," *National Geographic Traveler*, July/August 1991, 25.

Don't Grow Up

An astounding thing has been happening to me the last couple of years. People come up to me and say: "Are you still drawing the strip?" I want to say to them, "Good grief—who else in the world do you think is drawing it?" I would never let anybody take over. And I have it in my contract that if I die, then my strip dies. This is what my children want, too. They said, "We don't want anybody else drawing Dad's strip."

People also ask me if there's any message or theme to *Peanuts*. I suppose it might be that Charlie Brown, in spite of always losing, never gives up. But really, I never think about that. I just think about how I'm going to get two or three more good ideas. I draw from day to day.

You see, I work just as hard now, if not harder than I ever have. I think I'm more particular about what I do. My drawing is so much better now—in spite of the fact that I keep reading in articles that I'm not as good as I used to be, and that some people even say I should quit now before the strip deteriorates. But that's nonsense. I think that if a person maintains decent health and can handle the grind, then this is one of those professions where you should get better all the time.

My biggest worry is that I could use up my life. I could use up everything that I have experienced, all the thoughts that I've had about playing baseball when I was a kid and playing hockey and falling in love and being rejected, and all of the other things that happen to us throughout our lives. As you get older, you draw upon these experiences and use them all up until, finally, you're just doing the same things over and over and over.

I also have a great fear of becoming boring. There are a lot of boring people around, and unfortunately I think older people can become boring very easily. The way to prevent all that, I suppose, is by maintaining an interest in others and forgetting about yourself. It's a great crime to only talk about yourself all of the time and not express curiosity about other people.

I have found that simply asking other people about themselves can be quite fascinating. My wife, Jeannie, is good that way. It's a little sad, but I find that when she and I are out to dinner with other people, we seem to be the ones asking all the questions. We'll say, "Oh, where were you raised?" Or, "What did your father do?" And oftentimes when we get home at night, I'll say, "You know, Jeannie, you and I were the only ones that asked any questions. Nobody ever asked me anything."

I gave a lecture once, to a group of selected high-school students. I said, "Go home tonight and ask your parents where they met. Ask your dad what he did in World War II. Ask your mom if she went to the high-school prom. Talk to your grandmother, and don't just let the thing die, pursue the questioning. Do it now before it's too late." It's this kind of thinking that promotes cartoon ideas. Anybody can think of shallow cartoon situations, but I'm always trying to pursue something a little bit deeper. I suppose we're all at the mercy of the medium in which we work, and a comic strip doesn't give you that much room for a topic like death, but it can be there if you work at it.

I think you also have to make an effort to stay open to the world. I read a lot. I don't read simply for research or to get ideas; I read because I enjoy it. I took a college course in the novel a few years ago, and oddly enough I got an A in it. When I was a kid, I was a lousy student, the way Peppermint Patty is. I never knew what was going on, never did my homework, never did the reading assignments. This time I did all the reading and wrote a paper on Katherine Anne

COMES ANOTHER ONE...
! I LIVED PRETTY GOOD
THAT ONE...**THERE!**
T WAS A HAPPY SECOND..

6-4

THERE! OH, I WAS REAL
GOOD DURING THAT ONE..HERE
COMES ANOTHER ONE..

I CAN'T
STAND IT!

SCHULZ

Porter's book *Pale Horse, Pale Rider*. As I wrote it, I pretended I was writing for *The New Yorker*. Afterwards, the professor said to me, "I just want you to know that this is a perfect example of what a paper should be."

I also sit in front of the TV, but I don't really pay all that much attention to what I'm watching. I flip through all the channels. I'll start at 2 and go up to 60, and then when I hit *Northern Exposure*, I'll watch until Janine Turner is on. When she's not on anymore, I'll switch away again. (We almost met last year, but it didn't work out—and I was just crushed.) On the sitcoms, well, all everybody does is feed each other gag lines. They don't converse. Oh, and Jeannie and I always watch *Jeopardy* while we eat together. We try to get that last question. Once I was a whole category!

More seriously, I think that there is real danger of people thinking that what they see on TV is real life. From watching all the crime shows that are on these days, you get the impression that crime is all around us. Every time a woman pulls her car into a driveway, she's in grave danger. Crime just can't be *that* prevalent.

I've always liked the funny papers. I'm a great admirer of certain strips, like *Mutts, Rose Is Rose, For Better or For Worse*, and *Cathy*. I hold in complete disdain others that aren't any good or whose artists don't seem to be putting in the effort they should.

I think one of the other things that helps me keep in touch is the ice arena across the street, which I built 25 years ago. The place always has been a wonderful mixture of people, from little tiny kids up to old people. I go there every day, and I do hear things now and then. In fact, that's where I first heard the expression "Joe Cool," which is how Snoopy happened to become Joe Cool from time to time.

I never envision my characters growing old, though a couple of them have changed over the years. Charlie Brown, especially, has grown less sarcastic, more gentle. Sally has become much more important. She's developed a personality all her own. She's either very bright or very stupid. It's hard to figure out sometimes.

Maybe the real secret to not getting too old is not to grow up. I'm not a complete grown-up, really. I find that I still feel out of place most of the time. At different times I've had trouble traveling and become almost agoraphobic. I'm always insecure. I think I'll always be an anxious person. Somebody asked me in an interview recently, "What are you anxious about?" I said, "If I knew, I wouldn't be anxious anymore."

I have some very good friends in different professions, and I was just with four or five of them a couple of weeks ago. One of them was having a birthday, and we all went out to lunch. And I suddenly realized that I felt a little bit out of place. See, I'm not a businessman. I don't know anything about financial affairs or banking or what attorneys do or things like that. All I know is cartooning, golf, hockey, books and reading, and a few more things like that. So it's a joy to me when I find somebody that I can relate to.

I'm not Catholic, and I never will be, but right now one of my best friends is a Catholic priest. We play golf together every Thursday. And I have more fun with this guy, because he is extremely broad-minded. He knows my fondness for theological thinking and spiritual searching and all of that. And I can talk these things over with him.

Am I a religious man? I'll have to let someone else judge that. I'm a firm believer in the Kingdom of God, but I don't know about the afterlife—that baffles me. I think life is a total mystery. I have no idea why we're here, where it all came from or where we're all going, and I don't think anybody knows.

But here's one of the things that helps me, personally, to survive. Years and years ago, when I was living in Minneapolis, I met a man who played first viola for the Minneapolis Symphony. And in one of our talks he said to me, "You know, playing the viola to me is a lot like a religion." And I thought, that's nonsense. What does he mean by that?

But as the years went by, I could almost say that drawing a comic strip for me became a lot like a religion. Because it helps me survive

from day to day. I always have this to fall back upon. When everything seems hopeless and all of that, I know I can come to the studio
and think: Here's where I'm at home. This is where I belong—in this
room, drawing pictures.

Andy Meisler, "Don't Grow Up," *New Choices*, June 1995, 56–59.

My Shot: Good Grief!

Golf has always been a big part of my life, ever since I was eight years old, watching the Bobby Jones films at Saturday matinees, caddying at Highland Park in St. Paul, and eventually playing in what we still like to call the Crosby. I'm still sad that last week, for the first time in 37 years, I wasn't invited to play.

For a die-hard amateur such as myself, teeing it up on the Monterey peninsula with the world's greatest players was always a huge thrill. My first Crosby, in 1963, was the most memorable. I was paired with Peter Marich, and I shot 34—my best score ever for nine holes—on the front nine at Monterey Peninsula Country Club. Peter and I went on to finish ninth, the best I ever did.

I have so many wonderful memories from the Crosby. There was the birdie I made at Pebble Beach's brutal par-4 8th hole in 1981, and

the five-wood second shot to the 15 feet at Poppy Hills's par-5 12th in '93. (I missed the eagle putt, but we don't have to talk about that.)

I was so in love with the tournament that even quadruple bypass heart surgery didn't stop me from playing. I had the operation in September 1980, and five months later reported to Pebble Beach, where I learned that Kathy Crosby had paired me with Johnny Miller. It was the first time I had teamed with a superstar. "Anybody willing to play after having bypass surgery deserves a good partner," Kathy told me.

This year I'm told Snoopy was flying the MetLife blimp over Pebble Beach looking for me. Too bad I didn't get invited. I've been playing pretty well and might have won.

Charles M. Schulz, "My Shot: Good Grief!" *Sports Illustrated*, February 15, 1999, G9.

A Morning Routine

I usually drive to our ice arena in the morning, where I have an English muffin and some grape jelly and a small cup of coffee. I love to read the morning paper at that time of day. As soon as I get out of the car, there are two dogs who realize that it is me. They live in a rented house on the corner, and as soon as I begin to walk toward them, they come running to the fence. One is a huge black Lab and the other is a very small dog—not quite a beagle—but very small and perky, and they immediately recognize me. I don't know if it's the car they recognize or if it's me.

Our veterinarian says that dogs observe the way you walk, so there is something about my appearance, even from a distance, that they recognize. They know I have a doggie biscuit for each of them. As I approach the fence, the huge Lab jumps high in the air, bounding with great delight at the prospect of this cookie. The other little dog sometimes barks, but most of the time comes close to the fence with his tail wagging furiously.

I always talk to them. I always say, "Hi, dogs, how are you today? I got the cookies." I walk up to the fence and the little dog moves down the fence a little bit so the big one won't get too near him, and I lean down and I say, "Here is a cookie for the little dog." And then the big dog looks up at me and I give him his doggie cookie. What is so pleasing is that as he puts the cookie in his mouth, he looks up at me, and our eyes meet. There is something about this that brings great joy to me.

I then walk across the sidewalk to the arena where I have the English muffin and the cup of coffee. It is a highly recommended program that I would suggest to anyone. Either get your own dog or make friends with some neighborhood dog. You will find it extremely gratifying.

Charles Schulz, unpublished undated typescript.

Questions about Reading That Children Frequently Ask

#1 – *What was your favorite book as a child?*
It is difficult for me to single out one favorite book, as I have read and enjoyed many over the years. As I think back to some that I read as a young boy, one that comes to mind is *Hans Brinker* by Mary M. Doge. I have always been fascinated by ice skating and I think that it must have been a thrill for the kids in Holland to skate down the dikes.

#2 – *How does reading help with your career or hobbies?*
I am always looking things up and double-checking information. If I don't know something or I am not sure about something, I look it up or research it. Reading helps me to gain knowledge that helps me in creating my comic strip.

#3 – *What is your favorite book as an adult?*
I have read and enjoyed a great many books down through the years. One favorite is *My Last Million Readers* by Emile Gauvreau. I like this

book because it relates stories of early newspaper wars and beginning careers of various newspaper columnists and cartoonists. I have
always regretted that I never had the chance to meet the author.

#4 – *Who is your favorite author?*
F. Scott Fitzgerald. I have read almost everything Fitzgerald wrote
except maybe a few short stories. *The Great Gatsby* is one of my
favorite books, although it took about four readings before I understood it.

#5. *What advice would you give to our class about reading?*
Read, read, read! The more you read, the easier reading will become.
The more you read, the more knowledge you will gain, and finally,
reading is enjoyable. There are so many places you can visit, experiences you can experience and people you can meet, all through
reading!

Charles M. Schulz, "Questions About Reading that Children Frequently Ask,"
undated printed sheet.

MY
PROFESSION

Developing a Comic Strip

One of the hardest things for a beginner to do is merely to get started on his first set of comic strips. It is strange that most people who have ambitions in the cartoon field are not willing to put in the great amount of work that many other people do in comparable fields. Most people who have comic-strip ambition wish to be able to draw only two or three weeks' material and then have it marketed. They are not willing to go through many years of apprenticeship. Now, by this I do not mean that they are unwilling to serve the so-called "minor markets" of cartooning, but they are unwilling to draw the many, many cartoons that are necessary even before one can approach these minor markets.

It is strange that people in other areas of art are willing to paint and draw for the fun of it and for the experience involved, but very few cartoonists are willing to draw set after set of comic strips just for the experience. We seem to have a tendency to believe that all we have to do is perfect our lettering, our figure drawing, and our rendering, and then we are all set to go. Nothing could be further from the truth.

There is an area of thought training that has to be worked out. I think the beginner should reconcile himself to the fact that he is going to have to spend probably five to ten years developing his powers of observation and his sense of humor before he is able to venture into the professional side of the business.

Here, of course, I am speaking particularly of the humor strips. However, the same can be said of the adventure strips. The men

who write adventure strips are trained storytellers, and they did not arrive at this ability overnight. What, then, can we do to make our beginnings?

One of the main things to avoid is thinking too far ahead of yourself. Almost all of us have ideas which we think would be great for a comic-strip series, but when we attempt to break down these general ideas into daily episodes, we find it extremely difficult. This is where I think we should begin. Try to think of your daily episodes without concentrating too heavily on the overall theme of your comic feature. While you are concentrating on these daily episodes, trying to get the most humorous idea you can out of each episode, you will also be developing the personalities of your characters. You will find that ideas will begin to come from these personalities.

As your ideas develop personalities and as your personalities develop more ideas, the overall theme of your feature will begin to take form. This really is the only practical way to develop a good solid comic-strip feature.

If you go about it in the reverse manner, you are going to end up with weak ideas. You are going to be thinking so much about the general theme of your strip that your daily ideas will become diluted.

The system that I have recommended will also assure you of going in whichever direction your thoughts tend to take you. In these initial days of comic-strip work and practice, you must not confine yourself to any particular ideas. You must be in constant search for the characters and ideas that will eventually lead you to your best areas of work.

The characters that you start out to draw today may not be the same characters that you will end up drawing a month or year from now. New personalities will come along that you never thought of creating at the beginning, and frequently these new personalities will take you to completely different places. In regard to the characters themselves, it is not advisable to worry too much about their development. Let them grow with your ideas.

Remember, the one thing, above all, to avoid is the idea that you can think about this whole business for a long time and then suddenly one day sit down and draw 12 or 24 strips, send them in and expect to make your fortune. Some of the things about which I have been talking can be illustrated in the four strips that have been reproduced here. The ideas in each one of these depend upon the developed personalities of the characters involved. Right from the very beginning, we had established that Snoopy was a dog who could understand all of the things that the children were saying to him. He also has a very highly developed sense of intelligence and frequently resents the things that the children say about him. He definitely has a mind of his own and expresses it in thoughts and action.

Charlie Brown's personality goes in several directions. Most of the time he is quite depressed because of the feelings of other people about him, but at the same time he has a certain amount of arrogance. This is demonstrated in the strip concerning him and Snoopy. Generally, however, he is wholly struck down by the remarks of the other characters, especially Lucy. She represents all of the cold-blooded, self-sufficient people in this world who do not feel that it is at all necessary ever to say anything kind about anyone.

Schroeder is a rather innocent sort of fellow who is completely devoted to Beethoven and can sometimes serve as an outlet for the expressions of his friends, the way he is doing here for Charlie Brown.

I have always enjoyed working with Linus, who is Lucy's smaller brother, because I like to inject the naïve things that he frequently comes up with. None of these characters could have done or said any of the things in these four strips when it first began, for it took many months (and, in some cases, years) for them to develop these personalities. This is what I mean when I say you must be patient in developing your strip, and not to look too far ahead. Be perfectly content to work on the single strip that is now in place on your drawing board.

Students always seem interested in some of the practical points of reproduction that are involved in various comic strips, so I feel that I might comment somewhat on these. *Peanuts* always is drawn with four equal panels so that a newspaper editor can reproduce it in three different forms. He can run it horizontally, or he may drop one panel beneath another and run it vertically. Also, he may drop the last two panels beneath the first two and run the strip in the form of a square. Each one of the panels in these *Peanuts* strips is drawn 5½ inches high by 6½ inches wide in the original. This makes for quite a large panel, but I need the working space to be able to get the proper expressions and to make my lettering clear. *Peanuts* has a very great reduction and I have to work large in order that the pen lines can be made bold enough to stand this reduction.

I work exclusively with the pen and use the brush only to place the dark areas, such as we find here on the dog's ears, the brick wall, and Lucy's hair.

I think that design plays a very important part in the drawing of comic strips. Design involves not only the composition of the characters but the proper drawing of the other elements within the strip. I have tried to do this in the drawing of the brick wall by making the wall itself interesting and by varying the size and color of the bricks or stones in the wall. I have also tried to do this in the little bit of drapery that shows in the strip where Charlie Brown and Schroeder are talking. There is also a rather modernistic painting placed on the wall in order to give the strip a little extra design.

In the last strip, we have the corner of a house and the corner of a garage jutting into the panel to break up the square into pleasing areas. We also have the introduction of a little birch tree and a very small pine tree, which are good items because of their interesting designs. This is the sort of thing that you search for all your life, trying to develop to the highest degree.

Charles M. Schulz, "Developing a Comic Strip," written in 1959 for Art Instruction, Inc.

Peanuts—How It All Began

When I was growing up, the three main forms of entertainment were the Saturday afternoon serials at the movie houses, the late afternoon radio programs, and the comic strips. My dad was always a great comic strip reader, and he and I made sure that we always bought all four of the Sunday newspapers published in St. Paul and Minneapolis, Minnesota. I grew up with only one real career desire in life—and that was someday to draw my own comic strip.

Naturally, I was also a Walt Disney fan and could draw quite faithfully Mickey Mouse, Donald Duck, the three little pigs, and all of the other great Disney characters. I was also much impressed by Popeye and used to decorate the covers of my school books with drawings of that fabulous character. With me, it was not a matter of how I became a cartoonist, but merely a matter of when. I am quite sure that if I had not sold *Peanuts* when I did, that I would have sold something eventually, and that even to this day, if I had not yet sold something, I would continue to draw because I had to.

During the last year I was in high school, I began to take a correspondence course with Art Instruction School, which is located in Minneapolis. I completed their course in two years and then began to submit cartoons as all young boys do, but with no success. It was not until I returned from World War II that I made my first sale of some kid cartoons to our local newspaper in St. Paul. I also was finally able to break through in the *Saturday Evening Post* with about fifteen gag cartoons. And then one day in 1949 I sold *Peanuts* to United Feature Syndicate.

This is how it all happened, and if I look back upon it now, it all seems relatively simple. But I imagine this is because memory has a way of knocking off the corners.

There is no doubt in my mind that drawing a comic strip simply has to be the best job in the world. People send you wonderful letters, the syndicate for which you work sends you enough money to live on, and you are allowed to draw all of the pictures that you have been wanting to draw ever since you were a little kid. You also are given an outlet for all your emotions. From a practical standpoint, this is extremely important, for every emotion that you have, plus every experience and bit of knowledge which you have acquired, go into the creation of a comic strip.

A cartoonist really possesses a unique combination of talents. Actually, it does you no good to be able to draw too well or to become too educated. I have frequently referred to the comic strip as a sidewalk medium. By this I mean that the comic strip appeals to just plain people. However, if it is handled in the proper manner, a comic strip can burst these traditional bounds and appeal also to people who are better educated and fortunate enough to have a more cultured background. To do this, the cartoonist himself need not be extremely educated or cultured but he must possess that rarest of all commodities—plain common sense.

For those who are trying to get into the business, I would like to assure you that there is no "catch" to it. There is no definite series of steps which you have to take and you certainly do not have to have an "in" some place. All you have to do is be able to draw a comic strip which is better than any other now running. I do not even think that you have to worry about taking the strip to New York or wherever the syndicate may be located, because I am quite sure that submissions through the mail are examined just as carefully. When you submit through the mail, you give the editorial director the advantage of being able to study your work at his leisure.

The best bit of advice that I can give anyone is never to be caught without at least one iron in the fire. By this I mean you should always have something in the mail working for you. As soon as you complete a dozen gag cartoon roughs and send them off to a magazine, you should forget about them and begin to work on a newspaper feature. If it is a comic strip, as soon as you complete two or three weeks' material, mail it off to a syndicate and once again, forget about it. Immediately set to work on a panel feature, for instance, and then send that off while you are creating more gag cartoons. Always have something in the mail which is working for you. Also, do not ignore the minor markets such as your church publications or any small newspapers which may be published in your own home town. Do not make the most terrible mistake of all, which is to think that you will not give these minor publications your best work. In the first place, you will be robbing them of what they deserve from you, and in the second place, the ideas that you have now which you think are so good that they have to be saved or protected for better publications may not seem that good several years later. You will be surprised how much your ideas improve as you grow older. The ability to draw is not the only ability which improves with time. The ability to create ideas improves as you yourself mature.

Charles M. Schulz, "*Peanuts*—How It All Began," *Liberty*, Winter 1973, 14–16.

Creativity

Surroundings play a definite role in my kind of creativity. I have found from experience that it is best to work in one single place and have a regular routine. The beauty of the surroundings is not necessarily important. In fact, I feel more comfortable in a small, plain room than I do in a fancy studio.

My present studio is a very nice little building near the edge of Santa Rosa, California, and it suits our needs quite well. We have many people visiting us each week, and we need considerable storage space and a surprising amount of office equipment. When I first started drawing cartoons, it never occurred to me that I would someday need such things as typewriters, a Xerox machine, a postage meter, and all different types of stationary, mailing tubes, envelopes,

If we sell it, we'll print another.

and wrapping paper. There are five of us who work at the studio: two secretaries, an accountant, and the president of our firm, which we call Creative Associates. Evelyn Delgado and Pat Lytle are our two secretaries, and Ron Nelson is our accountant who handles all of my financial affairs. Warren Lockhart, the president, spends long hours helping our various licensees to work together and maintaining quality control. It would be very difficult for me to survive without the help of these people.

I have never had anyone work as an assistant on the actual comic strip or comic pages, partly because I feel that there would not be much for them to do. The drawing is relatively simple because of the style I have adopted, and I have too much pride to use anyone else's ideas.

Our day at the studio begins at 9:00 in the morning, but for myself, I find it very hard to get started until the mail has been distributed and I know if there are going to be any special projects for that day. That means that I rarely begin drawing until 9:30 or 10:00. I have also found as the years go by that I am getting to be a very slow starter. It is nice to come to the studio in the morning having at least one idea to draw, but if there is no such idea, then I have to get out my little pad of white paper and begin searching for something. Sometimes ideas come very rapidly but, unfortunately, there are also days when no ideas come at all. If I could know I was going to draw a blank day, then I would go off someplace and do something else. But I always hate to stop trying, so I sit there and make up little conversations with myself, thinking about the past, drawing Snoopy and the others in different poses, hoping something new will come along. There are days when I would like to draw something very philosophical and meaningful, something to touch the hearts of everyone, and find it absolutely impossible. One solution I use at these times is simply to get back to basics. Cartooning is, after all, drawing funny pictures, something a cartoonist should never forget. If a cartoonist remains within his own medium, if he does not let himself become carried too far afield and always remembers that his business is to draw funny pictures, then I believe he will have a minimum of bad days.

It is nice to be surrounded by reference books and be where it is quiet, but being in the same place each day is more important. When I first started drawing *Peanuts*, I was sharing an apartment with my dad on the second floor across the hall from a dentist's office and above a drugstore and liquor store. My dad's barbershop was downstairs and around the corner, making it very convenient for him to go to work each day. I used one of the bedrooms of this apartment as my studio and was quite proud of it. When I was first married, we lived with my dad and stepmother for a short time until we could complete preparations for a move to Colorado Springs. During this interlude, I basically drew the comic strip on a card table in the basement of my stepmother's home. In 1951 we moved to Colorado Springs, and I again tried to work at home in one of the bedrooms, but found it difficult to keep a regular routine. When I couldn't think of any ideas, it was too easy to find some distraction around the house. So I rented a small room in a downtown office building and worked there for almost a year. After we moved back to Minneapolis, I was offered a wonderful little room, which we liked to call my penthouse, at my former employer's, Art Instruction Schools. These were happy days for me, for I was back with my old friends and in the midst of those invigorating surroundings. Eventually, however, we made another move, this time to California, where, once again, I had a solitary place to work. The property we purchased had a studio on it, which had been a photographer's studio, and was all that any cartoonist could ask for. As the years went by and many changes took place among our friends and within our own family, my studio location changed again, and for approximately a year I actually worked in a small room over our ice arena. This became extremely difficult at times, however, for there were simply too many interruptions. We had to have a building completely to ourselves, so we built the structure I work in today.

I am not a very patient person when it comes to drawing pictures, which I have always thought was one of the reasons I became a cartoonist. An illustrator or a painter spends countless hours preparing his canvas, while the cartoonist merely reaches for a sheet of drawing paper. I do very little preliminary sketching and work directly upon the smooth-surfaced pen-and-ink paper, where the final drawing appears. I believe that as little pencil work as possible should go into the drawing, that the cartoonist should draw as much as is practical with the pen itself. I do not believe in the term "inking in." This would be an indication of merely following some prescribed pencil lines, with the inevitable results being less than the original sketch. Once I have thought of an idea, I can visualize the entire page. Sometimes, if there are as many as ten or twelve panels involved, it is necessary to start with the final panel containing the punch line, and number the panels backward in order to arrange the best spacing. Some ideas also require that the last panel be drawn first to eliminate any doubts as to the effectiveness of that final drawing. It can happen that I think of an idea, then discover that the drawing of that idea is really not practical, or maybe that it cannot be drawn as first visualized. It is far better to discover this by drawing the last panel first than after the entire page has been completed. The last panel in a Sunday comic strip is especially important. When the reader first glances at the Sunday pages of the comics, it is very easy for his eye to drop to the lower right-hand corner and have the whole page spoiled for him. Thus, it is sometimes necessary to try not to attract attention to that panel, to make certain that the beginning panels are interesting enough to keep the reader from skipping to the end. There have been times, for instance, when I wanted to use large lettering in the last panel to emphasize something being said, but decided not to for fear that the reader would be directly attracted to it and see the punch line too soon.

I do not prepare my continuing stories in advance, but usually let the daily episodes take a story where they wish to lead it. I find it is much more important to have a good series of daily ideas than to have a good story line. A comic-strip artist should never concentrate so hard on the story line that he allows his daily episodes to become weak. He should never let the reader feel that it is alright if he misses the strip for two or three days because he can pick up the story later on in the week. This is probably one of the worst things a cartoonist can do.

It took several years for me to develop the knack of present- ing short stories. I was already using themes and variations, but I believe it was the story of Charlie Brown getting his kite caught in the tree that started me off on these stories. He was so mad that he said he was going to stand beneath the tree, holding on to the string, and not move for the rest of his life. I then had the other characters come up to him, one by one, each day and either say dumb things to him, or something that would prompt him to answer in a sarcas- tic manner. It was a brief episode, but it did attract some attention and, I believe, new readers. Since then, I have tried to use stories frequently. I find it a good way to think of ideas because once a story gets going, all sorts of little episodes come to mind.

I don't know which story has been my favorite, but one that worked out far beyond my expectations concerned Charlie Brown's problem when, instead of seeing the sun rise early one morning, he saw a huge baseball come up over the horizon. Eventually a rash, similar to the stitching on a baseball, began to appear on his head, and his pediatrician told him it would be a good idea if he went off to camp and got some rest. Because he was embarrassed by the rash, he decided to wear a sack over his head. The first day of camp, all the boys held a meeting, and someone jokingly nominated the kid with the sack over his head as camp president. Before he knew it, Charlie Brown was running the camp and had the admiration of everyone. It seemed that no matter what he did, it turned out well, and he became known as "Sack" or "Mr. Sack," and became the best- liked and most-admired kid in camp. Unfortunately, he could not resist taking the sack off to see if his rash was cured, and once he had removed the sack, he reverted back to his old self. I don't pretend there is any great truth to this story, or any marvelous moral, but it was a neat little tale and one of which I was proud. Unfortunately, this kind of story does not come along very often, and I am satisfied if I can think of something that good once every year.

The longest series I have ever done involved Peppermint Patty and her ice-skating competition. I was able to stretch it out because it allowed me to go in several directions. First, there was the matter of her having to practice and of her involvement with her ice-skating pro, who was Snoopy. Then there was the making of her skating dress, as she talked little Marcie, against her will, into making the dress for her. I believe this story went on for five weeks and, of course, ended in disaster for poor Peppermint Patty, because the ice-skating competition for which she had prepared so diligently turned out to be a roller-skating competition instead.

Pacing is very important, and I usually go back to simple daily episodes after completing a story like this. Having many characters to work with gives you a broad keyboard on which to play, which I believe is important. I think that when you have done a story that gets close to realism, that involves the children themselves doing things that children are likely to do, then it is best, when the story is over, to do something as absurd as Snoopy typing his stories on his little typewriter, sitting atop his doghouse. Here, I am able to take part in a kind of humor that could not be done under regular circumstances. I can have Snoopy type outrageous puns in stories such as the one where he tells of the woman who is afraid to stay home while her husband goes on business trips. "I have solved our problem," the man said, "I have bought you a St. Bernard whose name is Great Reluctance. From now on, when I leave you, I'll be leaving you with Great Reluctance." This is the sort of pun that you would never draw under ordinary circumstances, but it works very well for Snoopy because it falls in with his personality. He has the right combination of innocence and egotism to make it work.

There is sometimes a great temptation to complete one or another of the running themes that are in the feature. It is always tempting to let Charlie Brown kick the football, or to give in and let Schroeder become Lucy's boyfriend. But this is something that has to be avoided. Charlie Brown can never be a winner. He can never win a baseball game because it would destroy the foundation of the strip. We cannot destroy the caricature of his personality any more than we can begin to modify some of his features to make him look more like a real little boy.

Some things happen in the strip simply because I enjoy drawing them. Rain is fun to draw. I pride myself on being able make nice strokes with the point of the pen, and I also recall how disappointing a rainy day can be to a child. When I think back to all those ball games that we looked forward to as teenagers, and how crushed we were if the game had to be postponed because of rain, it brings to mind emotions that can be translated into cartoon ideas.

I don't suppose a person has to be too psychologically observant to notice that boys play a more predominant role in *Peanuts* than do girls. I have always been self-conscious about this, but, after all, I know more about the suffering of little boys growing up than I do the suffering of little girls. I think the best of all was the one concerning ear piercing. Whenever I become involved in a story like this, I do enough research to make it authentic. Phone calls to several different physicians enabled me to find out the problems of having one's ears pierced and to obtain the opinions of doctors as to the advisability of the operation. I was also able to find out the problems of infection, pain, and other such things. It was a successful series, and one that I enjoyed as much as any.

Sunday pages and daily strips pose different problems. When I first began to do Sunday pages, I found the pacing difficult because I seemed to waste too much time getting my episodes started. Gradually, however, I began to see what the problem was and since then have learned to visualize a story or episode as a whole. I then chop off the beginning of that episode to make the action as concentrated as possible. In other words, with no time for the children in the strip to stand around in the first two or three panels, discussing what is going to happen, the action has to begin, in effect, in the middle of the episode, and to proceed rapidly. This would not be as true for a comic feature that involves more realistic characters, but it certainly is true for a strip like mine, which deals in abstract situations.

I have found drawing with pen and ink to be extremely challenging as well as gratifying. I feel that it is possible to achieve something near to what fine artists call "paint quality" when working with the pen. It is unfortunate that newspaper reproduction does not show off some of the good pen-and-ink or brush-and-ink work done by the better artists in our business. The rendering of a comic strip requires a good deal of concentration, and when drawing grass, for instance, I have discovered that I should be "thinking grass." If I am drawing the boards in a wooden fence, then I should be thinking of the texture of those boards if I am to achieve the appearance of that texture with the pen strokes. We used to have a little pen-and-ink exercise or demonstration that we sent out to the students at the correspondence school. We would draw three sets of pen lines, starting with a very fine set, progressing to a medium set, then ending with very bold lines. It used to be challenging to see how close we could get those pen lines to each other without having them touch, and to see if we could draw a perfect set. Doing this exercise hundreds of times helped me to develop the pen technique that I now possess. I abandoned the idea of drawing with the brush early in my career, even though I had experimented extensively with it and was reasonably pleased with the results. The characters in *Peanuts*, however, required a much tighter line.

As the years progressed and my style loosened considerably, the content of the strip, as I have tried to demonstrate, also changed. The important thing is that throughout the development of the strip, style and content have been consistent. I feel very strongly that a cartoonist should not overcaricaturize. The reader must be able to recognize the expressions on the character's faces, hence, the degree of caricaturization should not be so extreme that various proportions are distorted beyond recognition. Everything should be based on the way things actually look, and the degree of caricaturization should be consistent with the weight of the humor.

so involved with the characters in the strip that they will actually become disturbed if they think something bad is going to happen to any of them. In this case, Linus and Lucy were to move away from the town in which they had been born and raised. No one could quite believe that it was going to happen, and when they finally pulled away in their station wagon, it seemed to be a sad day for everyone involved. Soon the letters and telegrams began to arrive at the studio, and suddenly I realized I had made a mistake, for I had already decided that they would not be gone very long, that their father would change their mind and bring his family back to their old neighborhood. I wish now that I had had them stay away for at least a couple of months, but I guess I panicked out of fear that I would be seriously criticized by subscribing newspaper editors. At any rate, when I saw how concerned people really were, I knew I had a pretty good thing going. One doctor sent me a telegram that said: HEART-BROKEN OVER CURRENT DEVELOPMENT. BAD FOR PSYCHE OF YOUNG. PLEASE ADVISE. Another telegram said: PLEASE DON'T LET LINUS LEAVE. HE IS LIKE A SON TO ME. I answered that telegram by telling her, "Don't panic. Time heals all wounds." Another very nice girl wrote to me saying that she firmly believed that all 27,000 students at Berkeley were extremely upset. I especially liked the letter from the girl who wrote to say that her mother had a very insecure feeling about the whole situation and that if Linus and Lucy did not return to their old neighborhood, their whole family was going to crack-up. One young bible-college student from Oklahoma sent me a letter on which he had written in very huge letters the scream that I use in the strip so often—AAAUGH—and at the bottom he added the P.S.: "How many more sleepless nights must I spend wondering the fate of Linus and Lucy??—Help!" I also liked the postcard from Redwood City, California, which said, "Fear has gripped me at the breakfast table the last couple of mornings. I can't leave for work without knowing what is going to happen to Linus and Lucy." A girl from Stockton wrote, and after expressing her worry about the children she added the word "Sob," repeating it a hundred times at the bottom of the letter. Another very nice woman from Dayton, Ohio, asked me on a postcard in a most plaintive matter, "Why, why have you done this?" and then signed it, "In reverence for the departed." When the series ended, and Linus and Lucy had finally come back to their original neighborhood, several papers made it a front-page story and expressed their relief that the two characters were home. I received one particularly interesting letter from a woman who said, "Today, here in our household in Georgia, you have restored security and a sense of well-being."

I am not always prepared for some of the reactions that certain strips have brought. In 1970, Linus asked Lucy, "What would happen if there were a beautiful and highly intelligent child up in Heaven waiting to be born, and his parents decided that the two children they already had were enough?" Lucy replied, "Your ignorance of theology and medicine is appalling." In the last panel Linus said, "Well, I still think it is a good question." I was astounded when letters began to pour in on both sides of a subject that I had not realized I had touched. It was not my intention to get involved in a contraception or abortion debate. My point was simply that people all too frequently discuss things that they know little about. For the next several weeks I received letters complimenting me on my stand on population control, while I also received letters from readers who were fighting for abortion. Both sides were sometimes complimentary, sometimes critical.

Another Sunday page that stirred up far more trouble than I had anticipated showed Sally coming home and saying to her brother, Charlie Brown, that she had something to tell him but, evidently, did not want anyone else to hear. They went off by themselves and hid behind the couch in their living room where Sally whispered very quietly, "We prayed in school today." I have letters from people who told me that this was one of the most disgusting things they had seen in a comic strip, that they did not think it was funny and indeed thought it was extremely sacrilegious. Another woman, writing from West Orange, New Jersey said that she thought the page should be hung in the Hall of Fame, adding, "I think it is beautiful, and you have our heartiest support." This page, like the other, upset people on both sides of the subject, and also pleased people on both sides. Oddly enough, requests began to pour into United Feature Syndicate in New York to use reprints of the page to promote the fight to reestablish prayer in school, and the fight to eliminate prayer in school. The simplest solution was to deny everyone the right to reprint the strip.

In all the years I have been drawing *Peanuts*, I believe I have upset no other professional group more than optometrists. This is because every time any of the children in *Peanuts* have an eye problem, they always visit an ophthalmologist. The reason for this is that I have several friends who are ophthalmologists, and they have acquainted me with the nature of childhood eye problems. In 1966 I drew a series of episodes that showed Sally going to her ophthalmologist and having one of her eyes patched because "lazy eye" had been diagnosed. I immediately received angry letters from optometrists who said that she could just as well have gone to one of them as to an ophthalmologist. My research disagrees with them. However, they are still convinced that it was all a plot to discredit their profession, which, of course, is not true at all. I was concerned only for the children.

It is extremely important for a cartoonist to be a person of observation. He not only has to observe the strange things that people do and listen to the strange things that they say, but he also has to be reasonably observant as to the appearance of objects in the world around him. Some cartoonists keep a thorough file of things they might have to draw, such as a child's tricycle, or perhaps some kind of farming equipment. Other cartoonists do a good deal of actual sketching. This kind of observing has led me to something I can only describe as mental drawing, and at times that has become a real burden, for I seem to be unable to stop it. While I am carrying on a conversation with someone, I find that I am drawing with my eyes. I find myself observing how his shirt collar comes around from behind his neck and perhaps casts a slight shadow on one side. I observe how the wrinkles in his sleeve form and how his arm may be resting on the edge of the chair. I observe how the features on his face move back and forth in perspective as he rotates his head. It actually is a form of sketching and I believe that it is the next best thing to drawing itself. But I sometimes feel it is obsessive, like people who click their teeth and find that they have to do it in even numbers, or people who can't resist counting telephone poles. It may even be some kind of neurosis, but at least it accomplishes something for me.

If you should ask me why I have been successful with *Peanuts*, I would have to admit that being highly competitive has played a strong role. I am not one who will rage uncontrollably when losing at something, but I must admit that I would rather win than lose. In the thing that I do best, which is drawing a comic strip, it is important to me that I win. Each cartoonist fights for attention on the comic page. Some get it easily by being given more space than others, and some try to attract attention by using thick black borders around their panels, while some try for attention by using dramatic areas of solid black in their drawings. I was forced to present a strip that was the tiniest on the page, so I had to fight back by using white space. On a page jammed with comic strips, a small feature with lots of white space attracted attention. Once you get the attention, of course, you must retain it with the quality of your ideas, but that is your own responsibility. I hope that I am not the kind who grows bitter as the years take the inevitable toll on my career. I do know for sure that I work very hard to make my comic strip the very best one on that newspaper page each day. Whether or not I succeed is immaterial. I know that I really try. You could almost say that I view the comic page as a golf tournament or a tennis match, and it is important for me to be in the finals.

I still enjoy going to work each day, though friends who know me well can testify to the fact that I never actually use the term "work." If I have to say that I will not be free to do something on a certain day, I will always put it: "I have to go to the studio and draw funny pictures." It could be a superstition, but I guess it is really that I don't want anyone to think that what I do is that much work. It is one of the few situations in my life where I feel totally secure. When I sit behind the drawing board, I feel that I am in command. I am comfortable in my studio, and I am reasonably proud of many of the things that I have drawn. I think that I have done my share toward contributing to the advancement of our profession, and this also makes me proud. There have been a few regrets, of course. I think the fact that the *Peanuts* strip has always been printed so small (the size of the feature was developed to overcome sales resistance during a time of newsprint shortage) has contributed toward a dangerous and negative trend. Most comic features begin with just a daily run, and if that feature is successful the artist is rewarded with a Sunday page. There is a real struggle for the limited space that is available in the Sunday section of the average newspaper. Years ago, each feature covered an entire page of the newspaper. This space has shrunk, however, to half pages, one-third pages, and now quarter pages. This has made a mockery out of many otherwise fine features. It is like putting Cinerama on a ten-inch television screen. And just as I have resented the size that I have been forced to work in, I have resented the title *Peanuts* that was forced upon me. I still am convinced that it is the worst title ever thought of for a comic strip.

We have covered the world with licensed productions—everything from sweatshirts to lunchboxes to toothbrushes—and have been criticized many times for this, although for reasons that I cannot accept. My best answer to such critics is always that the feature itself has not suffered because of our extracurricular activities. I have drawn every one of the 10,000 strips that have appeared and I have thought of every idea. Not once did I ever let our other activities interfere with our main product—the comic strip. Our most severe criticism came when we took on the advertising account for the Ford Motor Company. For some reason many people thought this was too much, but I believe that the ads we turned out were of high quality and were dignified. Our television work has always received my closest attention, and we have even tried to watch carefully to see that we had sponsors who would retain the dignity of the feature. It has always been a mystery to me how we can be accused of overcommercializing something that is basically a commercial product.

But it really does not matter what you are called, or where your work is placed, as long as it brings some kind of joy to some person someplace. To create something out of nothing is a wonderful experience. To take a blank piece of paper and draw characters that people love and worry about is extremely satisfying. I hope very much that I will be allowed to do it for another twenty-five years.

Charles M. Schulz, *Peanuts Jubilee: My Life and Art with Charlie Brown and Others* (New York: Holt, Rinehart, and Winston, 1975), 157–80.

A Career in Cartooning

There is no form of entertainment that comes close to the sustaining power of the comic strip. Some of our most successful features have been running for as long as thirty to fifty years. This means that generations of people have grown up with the characters in the comic strip, and have learned to know them as well as their own friends. Readers demand the daily episodes with a fanaticism that is unbelievable until it is demonstrated or forced into the open by an editor who makes the dreadful mistake of leaving a comic strip out of his paper for one day only to find his switchboard deluged with calls, and as has happened, pickets walking back and forth in front of his building demanding justice. The terrible mortality rate of even some very good television shows has emphasized the staying power of the average comic strip. One reason for the comic strip's success in this area is, of course, the briefness of the episodes. Where television sets up contributors who try to turn out half hour and hour shows weekly, the comic feature requires only a moment each day. Beyond this, however, lies one of the great truths of artistic endeavor, the value of a single creative mind turning out a piece of work. Although many cartoonists employ assistants to help them with the various tasks of getting the drawings done, these are relatively mechanical, and invariably there is one creative mind responsible for each successful comic strip. Even the cases where we may have an artist-writer collaboration, we still are far away from the complicated team efforts that are necessary in other entertainment endeavors.

The establishment of a unique character seems to be the most important element in creating a successful comic strip. Even when the reader is unable to recollect humorous episodes that have amused him, he can still tell you all about the lead character in a comic strip, and if it is the sort that has a large cast of characters, he can tell you about each of them, and he will usually do so with real delight. A cartoonist's drawing style must be pleasing to the majority of readers, but one has only to glance through today's comic pages to discover that there is no formula for what is a pleasing style. Even what might be called good drawing is not necessary. The only quality that is really necessary is "effectiveness." The cartoonist must have a style that works. He must have a style that communicates. He can be literate, but he does not have to be a creator of great literature. In fact, if he can mirror the language of the man on the street, and match it with drawings that are compatible, he is bound to succeed. The best cartoonists are also those who recognize the importance of giving the reader a little something each day. It is fatal to let an episode drag, and it is fatal to imitate other mediums. The squares that make up a comic strip are not miniature movie or television screens, and they should not be treated so. A cartoonist must work within the confines of his own medium, and realize its limitations, one of which is obviously the rendition of scenes on a grand scale. There are things that cartoon characters can do, however, that live actors cannot, and these are the things that the prospective cartoonist must pursue. The act of a character flipping over backwards in the air is always effective. Wild expressions of joy, grief or despair can be depicted in a way that a real live actor cannot approach, and even the use of lettering in balloons for the dialogue in each strip, which on the surface, appears to be limiting, has the advantage of letting each reader give his own imagined tone of voice to the characters. How can a playwright go wrong when the audience is doing part of his work for him?

In the early days of cartooning, most of the artists got their start by working for a newspaper doing whatever chores were necessary

SCHULZ 11-5

or available. There was no real formula for judging what was good, and many wild and wonderful styles grew out of this vacant lot of pen lines. There was a certain roughness, at times even crudeness, that was quite admirable, for it has been lost today. In our era, the average cartoonist gets his start by selling to the magazine first, and here he all too often falls into the trap of imitating the host of cartoonists who draw the same type noses, half closed eyes, and smug expressions that we see in practically every magazine we pick up. The error here is compounded when the cartoonist gets the opportunity to draw a daily syndicated feature, but finds he cannot break out of the narrow confines of a branch of cartooning that demands anonymous characters. Thus, we have fewer real individualists than in former days even though we do have people drawing with smoother styles. The modern comic strip also suffers from a lack of space. It must be admitted that it makes the job much easier from the point of physical labor, but it also forces the cartoonist to work with less panels and almost no artistic variety. In the 1930's each Sunday comic took up an entire page of a newspaper. Now we find some pages holding three features in the same space, with the Sunday page becoming little more than an extended daily strip. All of this is due, of course, to syndicate competition and a situation where newspapers had too little space to give to new features because of a newsprint shortage directly following World War II. The newsprint shortage has abated, but newspaper syndicate is an organization without which the comic strip artist could not really exist. It markets and distributes the cartoonist's work for a share of the profits that usually amounts to fifty percent. There are many such organizations throughout the country, and they vary in size. Some have as many as forty or fifty different cartoon features which they sell to newspapers all over the world, while others exist on only three or four and sometimes even one. All, however, are constantly on the lookout for new material, and a beginner should never feel that the field is too crowded or that all the good ideas have been used.

There are other branches of cartooning that are as rewarding from a creative standpoint as the comic strip, and in some cases just as rewarding financially. Editorial Cartooning or Political Cartooning as it is most often called requires extreme dedication and more than a once-in-four-years interest in our national affairs. Only a few of our Editorial cartoonists are syndicated. Most of them work for individual papers, and most would stoutly deny that they are forced to adhere to the policy of the paper for whom they draw. An Editorial cartoonist with a few simple lines can clarify an issue that might never be possible to explain in a written column.

Magazine cartooning is a very broad field that extends from small publications who can pay only a dollar or two per cartoon to a few very sophisticated magazines that pay prices up to and over a thousand dollars per cartoon. This field is wide open to the beginner because the work is always bought on a free-lance basis. In the small markets the quality of the cartoon and its appropriateness to the magazine is what matters, not the artist's reputation or name value. Here the beginner should carefully select his markets and try to have something in the mail working for him at all times. A beginner can make no worse mistake than being caught without an iron in the fire which in his case is an envelope of cartoons in the mail.

The field of animation has changed so drastically with the coming of television in recent years that it is difficult to write about. Theatre cartoons are so expensive to make, and bring such slow returns that they have become almost nonexistent. Animation for television has developed in a variety of ways. Some of it is vastly inferior to what we knew during the days of motion picture cartoons, but none have adapted well to the new semi-action drawings, and have actually broadened the base of humor. The main producers of animated films are located in either Hollywood or New York, and many of them do very well turning out wonderfully inventive commercials for television without ever doing any entertainment-type films.

Cartooning as a whole is still one of the most fascinating businesses around. One can be the creator of a comic strip running in

500 newspapers or one can be an unknown amateur decorating a
letter to a friend in order to make it more meaningful. In either case,
the person doing the drawing gets the same satisfaction from putting down on paper something which he thinks is funny in a way
completely unique to his personality. He also knows that he is bringing a smile to someone somewhere, and there are few joys greater
than this.

Charles M. Schulz, "A Career in Cartooning," unpublished typescript dated
June 16, 1965.

Why 100 Million of Us (GASP!) Read the Comics

There is no field of entertainment that has such a large following, and yet has so little written about it as the comic strip. The daily and Sunday page comic strip artists get no reviews from discerning critics, and have only letters from readers and monthly statements from their various syndicates to tell them how they are doing. Thus, when a book is published that calls itself *The Funnies: An American* Idiom, edited by David Manning White and Robert H. Abel (Free Press of Glencoe, 1963), a host of cartoonists across the land rejoice to see that their neglected medium has been recognized.

As the preface states, this book "stems from a three-year inquiry into the whole nature of comic strips and their role in American life which was underwritten by a grant made by the Newspaper Comics Council, Inc., of New York to Boston University's Communication Research Center."

The regular reader of the funnies, of course, has no idea that such an organization as the Comics Council exists, and that it came into being when some people began to think that the funnies had lost their old-time appeal and were no longer attracting advertising. Most of us were under the impression that we were doing our job when we were drawing features that helped to sell the newspaper.

Nevertheless, in a fine report, which probably will not be of much interest to anyone outside the actual production end of the

REW
...

THEN I DON'T THINK IT'S FUNNY!

6-17

BIG SISTERS ARE THE CRAB GRASS IN THE LAWN OF LIFE!

SCHULZ

business, this book notes that "more than 100 million Americans, from the very young to the very old, read one or more comic strips in their Sunday newspapers, and, of these, about ninety million are regular readers."

For over 60 years the comic strip has fulfilled the very human desire of readers to tear aside sluggish description and get right to the dialogue. It has given those readers who are repelled by a huge book with no pictures, a story form that has a picture with every sentence, and action in every scene. Remarkably enough, it has also been able to attract those readers who are not repelled by pages of print and who are able to enjoy good reading, for Robinson and White tell us that the well-educated are consistent followers of the comics. In a chapter called, "Who Reads the Funnies and Why," they discover that "adults like to read funnies, but are ashamed to admit it. . . ." Apparently people also think that it is usually those on a lower educational or social level who read the funnies, and that they themselves are an exception.

"In our children's readership study, just the opposite was true. The children perceived the truth: the more highly-educated, the occupational elite are among the most avid readers of comics. Contrary to the general adult population's idea of who reads comics, the higher status group readers are the rule rather than the exception.

In order to make a book out of what was initially a report, several articles which are quite dated have been reprinted. Gilbert Seldes' famous discourse on *Krazy Kat* is very welcome, for it treats well what was probably the greatest strip ever drawn. Mr. Seldes, however, has not always been aware of other works of art that have been produced on the comic page, and here the authors have also failed us, for in their quest for illustrations to go with writing, they have not given us the work of enough of the original creators of such notable accomplishments as *Popeye*, *Bringing Up Father*, *Barney Google*, *Moon Mullins*, or *Polly and Her Pals*. Many of the men who have taken on these strips since the death of the original creators have done good jobs, but to give the modern reader no glimpse of the wonderful pen lines of these earlier cartoon geniuses is a mistake.

I, personally, also missed seeing a drawing of good old Captain Easy as originally done by Roy Crane. One of the real tragedies of our form of art is that characters such as Captain Easy go down to the most miserable of all deaths, dying day by day in the hands of those who try to perpetuate them.

An added torture is the placement of these characters into the hands of animation studios for afternoon television programs. The very short chapter "The Comics as Non-Art" proves nothing, and the two last chapters by Al Capp and Walt Kelly, good as they may be, have no place in this volume. They serve only to give you the feeling that the book didn't appear to look quite thick enough. Don't let this bother you, however, for this is still the best book of its kind ever written, and no one will be more happy to see it on counters everywhere than the cartoonists themselves.

Charles M. Schulz, "Why 100 Million of Us (Gasp!) Read the Funnies," *New York Herald Tribune*, June 5, 1963.

Happiness Is a Lot of Assignments

When Kirk Polking called to ask me to do this article, I was very pleased for several reasons. Ever since I was a teen-ager, I have been an avid reader of *Writer's Yearbook*, buying it each season, and devouring every word as I dreamed of the day when I would be drawing my own comic strip. Then, too, I felt it was about time that I cleared up some of the misconceptions that arose when the article appeared about us in the *Saturday Evening Post* (April 25, 1964). This article appeared to have been chopped up quite a bit, and out of this there came the impression that I was at my wit's end trying to survive all the pressures, and that my wife is a Lucy and that the people at United Feature Syndicate have no idea what is going on. Nothing could be further from the truth. Larry Rutman, Jim Hennessy, Harry Gilburt, and Jim Freeman of United are all men whom I regard as my friends, and we could have accomplished none of what we have if there had not been a very close working friendship. The only thing we have ever really disagreed on has been the title of the strip, *Peanuts*. (*Peanuts* was originally to have been called "Li'l Folks," but we found that Tack Knight had once used this title "Little Folks" so we had to come up with a new one. The only thing I could think of, and the one I still would prefer is "Good Ol' Charlie Brown," but this was vetoed by the syndicate, and from a list presented by one of their men, they picked *Peanuts* which I thought was terrible, and still do. It does not conform to the dignity I think the humor of the strip has.) It has become a running gag with us, but certainly no bitterness has ever developed. The important arrangements that had to be made when we negotiated the Ford advertising contract could never have been done by me. Only the experience of United Feature's Larry Rutman and Jim Hennessy made it possible. I also am not bothered by the pressures and my wife is no Lucy.

Many people seem to have received the impression that I am somehow attached to or even own Determined Productions which published *Happiness Is a Warm Puppy*. This again is a false assumption. Our happy arrangement with John and Connie Boucher, the real owners, came about because they drove up to my studio from San Francisco one day four years ago, and suggested that we do a *Peanuts Datebook*. It was out of the success of this initial venture that the later books were written and drawn. We had always had good success with our reprint books published by Rinehart and now Holt, Rinehart and Winston, but in the back of my mind there always was a desire to do more than just a reprint. Connie Boucher discovered three or four "happiness" ideas I had done in the daily strip, and suggested this be the basis of the book. I was rather doubtful that there would be enough material here to carry a complete book, but went ahead anyway, and no one was more surprised than I at its acceptance by the public. All of the projects with Determined have been fun because we make them fun. It is also exciting to do each new book in the face of criticism from other publishers who keep telling us that we should now be prepared for a flop because you simply cannot have two hits in a row, much less three or four.

The biggest subsidiary sale of *Peanuts*' career has been, of course, to the Ford Motor Company. All of the advertising has been handled by J. Walter Thompson Company, and here again the relationship has been friendly. Our only stipulation in this contract was that the characters in the *Peanuts* strip would have to retain their regular personalities, and this has certainly been done. I have also insisted on doing all the drawing myself because I feel that I am the only one who can draw Charlie Brown's head. We received quite a bit

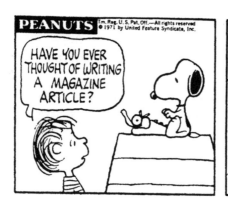

PEANUTS Tm. Reg. U. S. Pat. Off.—All rights reserved
© 1971 by United Feature Syndicate, Inc.

HAVE YOU EVER THOUGHT OF WRITING A MAGAZINE ARTICLE?

MAGAZINES ARE ALWAYS LO FOR "HOW TO" ARTICLES OR PE CONFESSIONS OR EXPOSE

of criticism when this project of putting out Ford ads first began. It was difficult to know just why, too, because commercialization of comic characters certainly did not begin with us. This has been going on since I was born. We could understand, however, the feeling of any newspaper editor who might be afraid that now, after all he had contributed to making *Peanuts* known through the medium of his comic page, we were going to run off and leave him with an inferior product as we gave our best to Ford. I think we have proved these fears to be false. I still regard the most important item on my drawing board to be today's strip. The managing editor is still our number one customer, and we are still in the business of drawing funny pictures to help sell newspapers. No subsidiary sales will ever take over this position.

Hallmark Cards has also done very well by us. And to reiterate, the relationship is a friendly one. Arnold Shapiro, their editor, goes over each new card idea with me, and I insist on drawing each one myself. This can be difficult when there are syndicate deadlines to meet, but it merely means learning how to pace yourself, and learning how quickly to get at the solution of problems. There is no time here for temperament. Drawings have to be done, so they are done. I am still amazed that a person gets his best ideas when he has the least amount of time, and how the days slip by with nothing being accomplished when there is too much time.

My religious teen-age cartoons are drawn first for *Youth*, the Gospel Trumpet publication in Anderson, Indiana. They are then let out to whatever other church publications want them, and this includes quite a list. My only stipulation is that they do not change any of the gag lines to suit their own needs. I preach in these cartoons, and I reserve the same rights to say what I want to say as the minister in the pulpit. I am a fanatic about this. In fact I am a fanatic about all my gag lines, and the way all my drawings are handled.

The usual process for these subsidiary sales is like this. (At least this is the way it works when I am contacted first.) Usually I get a phone call asking if I would be interested in using *Peanuts* in a certain way. (This, of course, eliminates the ones who call and refuse to tell you what their idea is over the phone because they are afraid you are going to steal it which I am not because it always turns out to be an idea for the manufacturing and selling of a Linus Security Blanket.) If the caller's idea has any merit at all, I tell him that he first has to clear it with Jim Hennessy at United Feature Syndicate. Then there must come the stern warning that he is not to call Jim and say, "Charlie is all for the idea, and wants to go ahead right away!" I find for practical reasons of business with United Features and just as important, for my own sanity, that it is best if I enter in no way into these negotiations until Jim has cleared all the financial arrangements. Then I am ready to find out what sort of art is required.

Last June we completed a TV documentary with Lee Mendelson Film Productions which I hope will be appreciated by all those who draw cartoons for a living. Besides telling the whole *Peanuts* story, we tried to show a day in the life of a cartoonist emphasizing the inevitable moments when you are alone with your creation. It took us almost a year to film, and should be shown sometime this season. The most difficult portions were the on-camera still drawings made to illustrate certain phases of my life. These were shot with the camera directly over my shoulder and under lights so hot that at one time a black crayon I was using actually melted before I could finish the cartoon. The best scene in the whole hour show was stolen away from me by Willie Mays. There is a beautiful shot of him drifting over to his left, and making a catch in center field to demonstrate to Snoopy how to catch. Snoopy then tries to imitate him, but catches the ball in his mouth. Afterwards, Willie says, "If I had to play for that Charlie Brown's team, I'd quit baseball!"

Each subsidiary sale we have made has come about because we thought it was one which did not cause our initial product, the *Peanuts* feature, to lose dignity. They have all been interesting projects, and many have brought in good sums of money, but the feature itself must always be regarded first. We are still in the newspaper business.

On Staying Power

A cartoonist is someone who has to draw the same thing day after day after day without repeating himself.

Sometimes there are days when ideas come very rapidly, but unfortunately, there are also days when nothing comes at all, and no matter how hard I try to draw something philosophical and meaningful, something to touch the hearts of everyone, I find it impossible.

At times like these, I never stop trying. I sit at my drawing board and make up little conversations with myself, searching my past for ideas, drawing Snoopy and the others in different poses, hoping something new will come along.

One solution I use when everything else fails is simply to get back to basics. Cartooning is, after all, drawing funny pictures, something a cartoonist should never forget. If a cartoonist remains within his own medium, if he does not let himself become too carried too far afield and always remembers that his business is to draw funny pictures, then I believe he will have a minimum of bad days.

I am not concerned with simply surviving. I am very concerned about improving. I start each day by examining yesterday's work and looking for areas where I can improve. I am always trying to draw the characters better, and trying to design each panel somewhat in the manner a painter would treat his canvas.

I am much more particular about ideas than I ever have been and almost never accept my first thoughts. More good cartoon ideas come out of a mood of sadness than a feeling of well-being. Several years ago, some events saddened me to such a degree that almost everything I

listened to sent me into a deep depression. In spite of this, I was still able to come up with ideas that were not only as good as anything I had ever done, but carried the strip forward into new areas.

If you are a person who looks at the funny side of things, then sometimes when you are the lowest, when everything seems totally hopeless, you will come up with some of your best ideas. Happiness does not create humor. There's nothing funny about being happy. Sadness creates humor.

In July 1981, I woke with a strange tight feeling in my chest. Quadruple bypass surgery followed. When I was admitted to the hospital, a nurse placed a large felt-tip pen nearby.

"Before you leave here, we want you to draw something on the wall," she said.

I am not one who goes around drawing pictures on walls. But I felt I had to fulfill this request.

Late one night during recovery, it came to me suddenly, like most cartoon ideas. I climbed carefully out of bed, picked up the pen and began to draw a series of Snoopys, showing him struggling with an inhalator to make the balls rise to the top. All patients could identify with this frustrating exercise. The last panel showed him collapsing with exhaustion and triumph.

Surgery was a difficult decision, but there I was, drawing, exhilarated knowing I had gone through something I had not been sure I was brave enough to attempt, and that maybe, drawing cartoons was what I was meant to do.

To have staying power you must be willing to accommodate yourself to the task. I have never maintained that a comic strip is Great Art. It simply happens to be something I feel uniquely qualified to do.

One of my favorite quotations comes from S. J. Perelman: "I don't believe in the importance of scale. To me, the muralist is no more valid than the miniature painter. . . . I think the form I work in has its own distinction, and I would like to surpass what I think I have done."

Charles M. Schulz, "On Staying Power," promotional poster for Panhandle Eastern Corporation, Houston, Texas, 1986.

Address to the National Cartoonists Society Convention

BRUCE BEATTIE, National Cartoonist Society President: I'd like to welcome all of you to the first of two wonderful seminars this morning. It's my hope that the seminars become a regular feature of this convention. I know that we all come here to socialize, but we are all resources for one another, and I think we ought to start taking advantage of that.

I can think of no person more qualified to be the leadoff speaker for this seminar program than Charles Schulz. He is the winner of two Reuben Awards, he has won numerous Peabody and Emmy awards, and he is the most widely syndicated cartoonist ever, with more than 2,300 newspapers. He has had more than 1,400 books published, selling more than 300 million copies in 26 languages—it's just an extraordinary legacy.

This all began about a few months ago when he was going to meet with me and [my wife] Karen at his Santa Rosa studio. I had expected to meet Charles Schulz for about 15 minutes; I had expected that we would have a couple of photos taken, and then we would be shuffled out the door. Instead, he spent the whole day with us. During the course of that day I began to get to know Sparky, and what impressed me about him was, after all of his accomplishments, he is still a cartoonist who is doing his daily cartoon. He goes into work every day like us beginners, and what really impressed me about him was the passion and dedication he has for the work and the enthusiasm he has for his work. This is something some of us, I think, lose at times. We all want to become rich and successful, and sometimes we lose sight of the fact that what it is all really about is cartoon art.

In short, I came away that day with Sparky an inspired cartoonist. I really mean that. That's why I want to have him start the seminar program today, and I'm hoping that maybe a little of the inspiration he gave to me will rub off on you.

CHARLES SCHULZ: Last month, [my wife] Jeannie and I took a trip, and I played in the Dinah Shore golf tournament, and about the second or third evening they had a buffet dinner. We brought our food into a room and sat down at a round table and we introduced ourselves around. At one point, an elderly woman sitting on my left said, "'Charles Schulz'—that's kind of a nice name, isn't it?" And I said, "I never really thought about it." And she said, "Isn't that the name of the fellow who's the cartoonist?" Then she said, "He's dead, isn't he?"

To compound the problem, three nights ago, some of the people from United Media dropped by Santa Rosa, and we all went out to dinner. Afterwards, we were passing out through the entrance, and the man at the counter stopped me and said, "There's something I want to tell you—there were two or three ladies in there the other night who got into a big argument. One of them said you were dead, the other said, 'No, he's not!'" Well, even though I've been drawing for almost 45 years, I'm still here!

Back when I used to work at a [cartoon] correspondence school, Art Instruction Inc. [in Minneapolis], it was a wonderful place to get started because the atmosphere was not unlike that of a newspaper office. All the instructors were very bright people; they were all ambitious, each of them had his or her desire whether it was to

be a fashion artist, or a cartoonist, or a painter. There was Walt Wilwerding, the portrait painter; Frank Wing, the old-time cartoonist, sat right in front of me, and he was the one who taught me if you're going to draw something, draw it from life first—you can't cartoon something until you know how to draw it accurately first. Anyway, he did a lot for me. Once I got started on the [*Peanuts*] strip I liked working there, because I could go downstairs to the stockroom, and I could find nice pieces of cardboard and wrapping paper, and they gave me a room to work in after I quit the job as an instructor. I used to go down, get the cardboard, fold my strips in half, and then I'd wrap them up and take them to a little subsidiary postal office— and I did this for several weeks. One morning, I went in there, and [the postal worker] looked at me, and the package, and he said, "You come in here every week, and this says 'United Feature Syndicate'— what is that?" I said it was a newspaper syndicate, and they distribute and sell comic strips. "Like *Dick Tracy*?" he asked. And I said, "Well, yeah, something like *Dick Tracy*." And he said, "Well, where's your Cadillac?" I said I didn't have a Cadillac, and he asked what was it I did draw. "It's that little strip that runs in the evening paper about this kid and his dog"—I never use the name *Peanuts*, because I hate it—and he said, "Oh, I'll try to read it." So the week went by, I drew another batch of strips and I took them down and handed them in to be mailed out, and he looked at me and said, "Oh, I read your strip last night—I didn't think much of it."

I was reminded of that incident because a couple of weeks ago—I usually work until about 4 o'clock in the afternoon. I just can't stand sitting there any longer; I always like to drop into a bookstore and see what new things they have. As I was pulling out of the driveway I was thinking that this was a good batch of strips that I drew. And I can honestly say that I still get just the same thrill at the end of the week when I have drawn that thing from Monday through Saturday, and I feel that I've thought of some pretty good ideas, and they've been drawn the best I can draw them, and it's a nice feeling to know that they're going to be mailed out and that I have done it again.

Because back in Minneapolis, when I went to that little post office, I had the same feeling—that I had done a good batch of strips, to wrap them up and mail them in and know that I had something the best that I could do.

So the feeling is still there, and I guess it's going to be 45 years next year, and I can absolutely guarantee you that despite what some columnist for the *Chicago Tribune* wrote a few years ago, that it's time for me to retire, that the strip is not good any more, that the strip has lost all meaning and everything, I work harder now—I truly do—I am more particular about everything I draw than I have ever been. I almost never send in anything that I'm not totally pleased about. And I am still searching for that wonderful pen line that comes down—when you are drawing Linus standing there, and you start with the pen up near the back of his neck and you bring it down and bring it out, and the pen point fans out a little bit, and you come down here and draw the lines this way for the marks on his sweater, and all of that. . . . This is what it's all about—to get feelings of depth and roundness, and the pen line is the best pen line you can make. That's what it's all about.

If there's somebody who is trying to be a cartoonist, or thinks he is a cartoonist, and has not discovered the joy of making these perfect pen lines, I think he is robbing himself—or herself—of what it is all about. Because this is what it is! The times you make these wonderful pen lines, and make them come alive. I tell people when they ask me that the most important thing about a comic strip is that it must be fun to look at. If you are drawing something day after day after day, no matter how funny the dialogue might be, it still must be fun to look at. If the reader picks it up, the reader may know absolutely nothing about drawing, but the drawing must be fun to look at. I think that's very important.

Years ago, I used to gather now and then with some people from around St. Paul-Minneapolis and talk about cartooning, and every time I would read essays by other people who were more or less trying to get started, I used to see the phrase, "This crazy business about slinging ink." This is not a crazy business about slinging ink. This is a deadly serious business. I've always had a wonderful relationship with my editors, starting with Jim Freeman, working on up, and now I have the best editor that I've ever had, Sarah Gillespie. I've always had a good relationship with the men who were the sales managers and the salesmen, and the men who were the presidents of the syndicate, starting with Larry Rutman, who treated me like a son. Now, I think it's important for all of us and all of you to establish those relationships. But it's not a business of slinging ink. It's a deadly serious business. And someplace up there [in the corporation], there are some people that you will never know existed. They don't care anything about you—so watch yourself. They don't even read the comics. They could not possibly care less what happens to you. Sarah Gillespie cares about what happens to you, [and some others do]; I don't know who these people are "up there," but I'm sure that every organization has this group of mystery people up there. They are like the people who own a ball club, like the man who owns a theater—he doesn't really care about the actors. He likes the bottom line and all that. Those are the people to watch out for. The older you get—well, it took me 40 years to discover that.

I think one of the most dangerous things, as you draw day after day after day—and as long as I'm standing here, it's about time; I might as well slip this in—Don't let them kid you that this is a business that has so much stress that you have to have time off. I was talking to a friend the other day, and I said, "You know, cartoonists have nothing to complain about. This is what we've wanted to do all of our lives, and we finally have a chance to do it, we can live anyplace we want to, we can work any hours we want to, and they send us money." Anyway, anyone who doesn't want to join the National Cartoonists Society is baffling. Someone says he's not a joiner? I'm not a joiner either, I don't belong to anything, but I think we all have an obligation. You know the person you have an obligation to? It's the salesman driving around in his Dodge trying to sell your strip all the time. For five years, trying to get some editor, who finally says,

Crane! Percy Crosby used the most wonderful pen lines you've ever seen in your life, and if you're a young person and you haven't studied Percy Crosby, you'd better get down and find some books and see how Percy Crosby drew. Al Capp, of course, and all the wonderful characters he created. They were all drawn in kind of a mild form of caricature: If the readers can't tell where the eyes are and where the nose begins and where the mouth is, you're in real trouble because that character, with that type of cartooning, can never show any emotion. So you've got to show them where the eyes are, where the mouth and the nose are. You can get away with a greeting-card kind of cartooning, but you're not in greeting-card cartooning. You're in cartooning, drawing people with some kind of emotion. And this is why I believe in the mild form of cartooning. Show them where the mouth is; show them where the eyes are and the nose is. But, if the cartoon character says something, don't have the character emote with a great, big expression over some very mild statement. It's better to just leave out the character completely if you're not sure how that person would react, and just go to a close-up of somebody's face or something. But I hate this business of overreacting to something like that.

Somebody mentioned the other day that on a Sunday page, it's not a bad idea to draw the next-to-the-last panel first. It's terrible when you draw a whole Sunday page and find out that it's not going to work. I read that Ernie Bushmiller used to do that. It's something that I discovered on my own. Now, as your strip develops, I think you will find, too, that all comic strips have a single character around which all the others revolve. Mort Walker has done this with Beetle, Walt Kelly did it with Pogo; and usually the main character is a person with kind of a mild personality. He has some quirks and all that, but it's the character the strip revolves around that's so important. You can go back to Al Capp and Li'l Abner. And I think this is very serious—as the years go by, it's very important to build up a cast of characters so you can have a change of pace. I think a change of pace is really important. I think it's important, if you're doing a ridiculous strip, to throw in some serious material now and then. Fortunately, I can do a lot of the corny things with Snoopy, like when he writes, he thinks his writing is great, but it's terrible! But you couldn't get away with that if somebody else was doing the writing. So I think that is very important.

Now, we're all different; we come from different backgrounds, obviously. We all have different ambitions. I read a lot, and I pick up bits of information here and there, and these are things that sometimes provide wonderful ideas. Did you know that if you go into a pitch-dark room—you should try this sometime!—and chomp down on a wintergreen Lifesaver, it makes sparks? Judy Sladky, the world-famous skater who does work as Snoopy, was out at Christmas and told me this; I said, "That's crazy! That doesn't work!" So I go into a dark room, chewing on wintergreen Lifesavers, and I couldn't make them spark. And it's hard on the teeth. So I drew a series where Snoopy, the world-famous guide, was taking Peppermint Patty and Marcie on a walk through the woods and they get lost, and it's hard and they have no flashlight, so they promptly found their way back home by chewing wintergreen Lifesavers. They followed the sparks as they went through the woods.

The first thing I do when I draw a Sunday page is I take out a *Peanuts* calendar and I find out when the page is going to appear. Once last year, lo and behold, I looked at it and it says June 6. I had forgotten all about D-day the previous year. So it was a total accident that I happened to discover that that Sunday was going to come out on June 6. So I drew one huge panel, which I never used to do. Snoopy is landing at Omaha Beach, and he's lying in the water, just his head and the helmet amid all the things Rommel had put down there to keep the soldiers from landing, and down below I just wrote, "June 6, 1944—To Remember." And I got such a wonderful response from men all over the world. Now, I realize that this year is the fiftieth anniversary. I beat myself by one year! Now, I can't let these men down. I've been thinking for a whole year about what I'm going to do for D-day, the actual landing. They're going to be having these celebrations in France, 70-year-old men are going to jump out of airplanes again. And somewhere I read—but how many people know this? This is a good trivia question—does anyone know when Erwin Rommel's wife's birthday was? It's not that hard a question, if you think about it. Erwin Rommel's wife had her birthday on June 6! Now Rommel knew this, of course, and several weeks before, he had planned to go ahead and go home for her birthday. He had already bought her a pair of blue suede shoes in Paris, and he figured the Allies were not quite ready to land, according to their studies. He felt there was time to go home. So he went home for her birthday, and they landed while he was gone! It was a tremendous stroke of luck for the invaders. Now, that's a pretty good idea, but how do we make it work? I could have Snoopy think about it, but he can't talk to anybody, even though he knows it. I thought maybe he could be sitting in a pub with Peppermint Patty, but how could he tell her that Rommel's not going to be there? This is a secret. Well, I could have him talk to Marcie, but I wanted to save Marcie in case, after he lands, he could meet her as the little French girl. He always goes over to her house to quaff root beers—and it turns out he's not in a little French café, he's in Marcie's kitchen drinking root beer, much to the annoyance of her mother, because here's this dog in her kitchen. So that didn't work either. I kept thinking about this week after week, until one day all of a sudden it hit me—why not have Linus give a report? So we start off with Linus standing in school, saying, "This is a report on D-day," and he talks about the invading forces being prepared to move, but nobody knows when, except one unknown GI. Snoopy's sitting in his pub, and all of a sudden he gets the note: Rommel's not going to be there; he's gone home because of Mrs. Rommel's birthday. And Linus says, "This unknown hero rushes off, calls General Eisenhower, and says that 'Tomorrow's the day you have to invade because Rommel won't be there.'" But how are we going to do that, because Snoopy still can't talk?

So I think about it, and finally I get the idea that Linus says, "When he ran off to call General Eisenhower, he spoke in code." The last panel shows one of those old English phone booths, all painted red, and I couldn't find out what the telephone looked like inside the phone booth, so I just drew the phone booth, kind of blacked in the windows; and we see the last panel, just a phone booth, and the word balloon that says, "Woof!"

I followed that up with five dailies where he actually lands at Omaha Beach. "Here's the world-famous GI crashing through the surf, charging up Omaha Beach," and for the first time in my career, I used Crafting Doubletone [shading paper], and I called Sarah Gillespie to warn her that I'm not going to do this all the time. I just wanted it for scenes like that, which would give it a real splashing up through the surf in one long panel, and there a small panel at the end where Marcie's on the phone, and she says, "Hey, Charles, your dog is over here, and he's running back and forth in my wading pool." Again, I needed an angle, and so each time I show Snoopy in his imagination doing something, then it's explained by somebody in the other panel about what we're seeing.

I think comic strips should live a life of their own. Don't get involved too much with television. You have to show characters watching it, because it's part of our lives. But whatever you do, don't use expressions that have become famous on television. You are out here to create your own language and your own expressions. You are creating in a media just as good as anything they do on television. We can do things that live actors can never do. A live actor could never pull a football away and show Charlie Brown up in the air and landing flat on his back. These are things they could never do.

We have to stay within our medium, so I say don't rely too much on watching television, and trying to make comments on things you see on the screen there. There are wonderful things in *Bartlett's Quotations*, little bits of poetry and such. I always like the one from either Tolstoy or Scott Fitzgerald—I don't know who it was—"In the real dark night of the soul, it is always three o'clock in the morning." That's a real cartoon idea for your characters.

Which again brings us back to the point you have to have characters that can do lines like this. If they are overly caricatured, they cannot talk like this. I don't know how many ideas I've done with poor Charlie Brown lying in bed. "Sometimes I lie awake at night and I ask, 'Is it all worth it?'" And then a voice says, "Who are you talking to?" And another voice says, "You mean: to whom are you talking?" And Charlie Brown says, "No wonder I lie awake at night."

"Sometimes I lie awake at night and I ask, 'Why am I here?'" And a voice says, "Where are you?" "Here," Charlie Brown says. "Where's here?" says the voice. "Wave your hand so I can see you." Charlie Brown says, "The nights are getting longer." "Sometimes I lie awake at night and I ask, 'Why me?'" And the voice says, "Nothing personal—your name just happened to come up."

I guess I talked infinitely longer than I'd planned, but I'd love to answer any questions you may have.

[Following are responses to questions and comments from the audience.]

[About retirement] When I quit, retire or die—like those two women thought—well, we had a big meeting with all the attorneys and my own children, and they said, "We don't want anyone else drawing Dad's strip." So that's it.

[About his statement once that "there will always be a place for inno-cence"] I have never done anything that I consider the least bit offensive. There are no fire hydrants in my strip, no toilet bowls. There is a market for innocence. I told this to Lee Mendelson way back

when we first started doing television shows. There's still a market for things that are clean and decent.

[*About the origins of the Peanuts animated cartoons*] A man from Coca-Cola called Lee Mendelson and said "We're kind of looking around for a Christmas show. You don't have any ideas for us, do you?" And Lee told them, "I think we might." So Bill [Melendez] and I got together one night and wrote the Christmas story. And it was in the midst of deciding what would happen, I said, "Gee, Bill, we can't get around it—if we're going to do a Christmas story, we have to use the famous passage about the baby Jesus." And we did. Linus walked out and said, "Lights, please!" And he recites the wonderful passage. No one had ever done this sort of thing before. And we did it.

[*About comic character merchandising*] I don't know Bill [Watterson]. I've never talked to him. I wrote a foreword for one of his books, but I've never talked to him. Like I said before, we're all individuals, and I dreamed of becoming a comic strip artist. I never thought about licensing or anything like that, but I was driving down the street one day and I saw a truck that had Yosemite Sam pasted on the back of the truck. And I thought, "People love cartoon characters, and the man who drives this truck loves Yosemite Sam enough to paste his likeness to the back of his truck." What in the world is wrong with that? People love coffee cups and things, and if you can put the characters on TV, sometimes it's just terrible, but if you can do it [well], fine. *You're A Good Man, Charlie Brown* is the most-performed musical in the history of the American theater, because we did it right, and I don't see anything wrong with that. Plus, I don't think I'm a true artist. I would love to be Andrew Wyeth or Picasso . . . but I can draw pretty well and I can write pretty well, and I think I'm doing the best I can with whatever abilities I have been given. And what more can one ask?

[We create] a commercial product; we help the newspaper editor sell his paper, and I don't think what I do is so great that . . . 20 years ago in an interview with *Playboy*, Al Capp said, "*Peanuts* has just about run its course now. . . . Little kids talking like adults—these little kids don't talk like adults. Adults don't even talk like that!" Anyway, that was 20 years ago, and since then I've added 1,500 newspapers.

Delivered May 14, 1994.

Pleasures of the Chalk-Talk

As a general rule, I must admit that I am not overly fond of giving chalk-talks. I always enjoy myself while I am actually performing, but after it is all over, and I have loaded my equipment back into my car, I suddenly find myself with that long lonesome drive home, and I wonder to myself, "Why in the world did I do this?"

Well, let's talk about the "why" for a moment. One reason, and the most important, is a feeling of gratitude for being able to make a living doing something you enjoy so much. Somehow, this seems like a way to repay for this great gift that has been given to you. It is also a good way to take some program chairman off the hook, especially if he is a friend of yours. But it is no easy task. In practically every appearance I have made there has been someone in the audience who has sat silent throughout the entire show, and while you are standing there drawing those silly pictures and doing your best to make everyone laugh, this one person just sits there like he or she couldn't care less. This usually makes you wonder "why" you agreed to come.

I prefer to work with a huge easel, a black crayon, and a microphone that can be placed to one side of the board so that I can stand away from the drawing after it has been made and talk about it. I hate after-dinner speeches in halls that extend so far back you cannot reach your audience. I much prefer a close-in group that has come especially for this event. I refuse to try to follow a Barber Shop Quartet or a magician or a ventriloquist, for they have whipped the mind of the audience to a level where my talking quietly of the problems of Charlie Brown is a sure let-down.

As an opener, I have found that a drawing of Charlie Brown in his big baseball hat wearing his over-sized glove is still the best one I have ever come up with. It is an adaptation of a gag cartoon I sold to the *Saturday Evening Post* back in 1949, and after talking about all of Charlie Brown's problems I wind up the bit by saying, "Even though he takes quite a beating he still feels that he has the most important position on the team because he stands here to see that the ball doesn't roll down the sewer!"

The secret to this whole situation, of course, is that no one has really recognized what it is that I have drawn behind him until I finally mention the word "sewer." I can usually judge pretty well what sort of evening or day it is going to be, too, as I start to draw Charlie Brown's head. If giggles begin to run through the audience as soon as I draw that round head and innocent face, then I know that I am in, and we will have a good time. My procedure is to go on from there drawing each character in the *Peanuts* strip, and talking a little about his or her personality. I enjoy a group where we can have questions and answers afterward because this is both fun and a good way to pace your talk. The sample drawings shown here are drawn exactly as I would make them with a black crayon before a live audience. No preliminary pencil work is ever done.

Charles M. Schulz, untitled and unpublished typescript.

MY
ART

The Theme of *Peanuts*

The initial theme of *Peanuts* was based on the cruelty that exists among children. I recall all too vividly the struggle that takes place out on the playground. This is a struggle that adults grow away from and seem to forget about. Adults learn to protect themselves. In this day of organized sports for children, we forget how difficult it once was for smaller children to set up any kind of ball game at a playground because so often there were older and bigger kids to interrupt the fun. I have always despised bullies, and even though someone once suggested that I have much psychological bullying going on in *Peanuts*, I do consciously try to stay away from that sort of thing.

As the strip progressed from the fall of the year 1950, the characters began to change. Charlie Brown was a flippant little guy, who soon turned into the loser he is known as today. This was the first of the formulas to develop. Formulas are truly the backbone of the comic strip. In fact, they are probably the backbone of any continuing entertainment. As Charlie Brown developed, so did characters such as Lucy, Schroeder, and Linus. Snoopy was the slowest to develop, and it was his eventually walking around on two feet that turned him into a lead character. It has certainly been difficult to keep him from taking over the feature.

There are various origins for the characters. Charlie Brown is supposed to represent what is sometimes called "everyman." When I was small, I believed that my face was so bland that people would not recognize me if they saw me some place other than where they normally would. I was sincerely surprised if I happened to be in a downtown area of St. Paul, shopping with my mother, and we would bump into a fellow student at school, or a teacher, and they recognized me. I thought that my ordinary appearance was a perfect disguise. It was this weird kind of thinking that prompted Charlie Brown's round, ordinary face. Linus came from a drawing that I made one day of a face almost like the one he now has. I experimented with some wild hair, and I showed the sketch to a friend of mine who sat near me at Art Institute whose name was Linus Maurer. He thought it was kind of funny, and we both agreed it might make a good new character for the strip. It seemed appropriate that I should name the character Linus. It also seemed that Linus would fit very well as Lucy's younger brother. Lucy had already been in the strip for about a year, and had immediately developed her fussbudget personality. We called our oldest daughter, Meredith, a fussbudget when she was very small, and from this I applied the term to Lucy. Schroeder was named after a young boy with whom I used to caddy at Highland Park golf course in St. Paul. I don't recall ever knowing his first name, but just Schroeder seemed right for the character in the strip, even before he became the great musician he now is.

One night, over ten years after I began drawing *Peanuts*, I had a dream in which I created a new character whose name was a combination of Mexican and Swedish. Why in the world I had such a dream and would think of such a name as José Peterson is a mystery to me. Most of the time, things that are a complete riot when you are dreaming are not the least bit funny when you wake up. In this case, however, it seemed like a good idea, so I developed a story about the arrival of José Peterson in the neighborhood, and he has remained ever since, usually playing on Peppermint Patty's baseball team.

Patty has been a good addition for me, and I think she could almost carry another strip by herself. A dish of candy sitting in our living room inspired her name. At the time I was thinking of writing a series of children's books completely separate from the *Peanuts* strip, but my schedule kept me too busy to ever get started and almost a year went by before I decided that I had better use this name, lest someone else think of it and beat me to it. So in this case I created the character to fit the name, and Peppermint Patty came into being. Her little friend, Marcie, who is always addressing her as "Sir," has also been a good addition to the strip.

I have always believed that you not only cast a strip to enable the characters to do things you want them to, but that the characters themselves, by their very nature and personality, should provide you with ideas. These are the characters who remain in the feature and are seen most often. The more distinct the personalities are, the better the feature will be. Readers can then respond to the characters as though they are real.

It is interesting to observe that many of the lead characters in our most successful comic strips have had similar personalities. Readers are generally sympathetic toward a lead character who is rather gentle, sometimes put upon, and not always the brightest person. Perhaps this is the kind of person who is easiest to love. I really don't know. It may also be that giving the supporting characters the most distinct personalities makes for a more controllable story. A character with more of a "middle ground" personality can hold the rest of the group together. In the case of *Peanuts*, I like to have Charlie Brown eventually be the focal point of almost every story. No matter what happens to any of the other characters, somehow Charlie Brown is involved at the end and usually is the one who brings disaster upon one of his friends or receives the brunt of the blow. Charlie Brown has to be the one who suffers, because he is a caricature of the average person. Most of us are much more acquainted with losing than we are with winning. Winning is great, but it isn't funny. While one person is a happy winner, there may be a hundred losers using funny stories to console themselves.

Snoopy's appearance and personality have changed probably more than those of any of the other characters. As my drawing style loosened, Snoopy was able to do more things, and when I finally developed the formula of using his imagination to dream of being many heroic figures, the strip took on a completely new dimension. I had observed that there were many neighborhood dogs that seemed almost smarter than the children who were their masters. The dogs seemed to tolerate the silly things the kids did; they seemed to be very wise. This was one of the initial themes of Snoopy that I have built upon in many ways. Snoopy refuses to be caught in the trap of doing ordinary things like chasing and retrieving sticks, and he refuses to take seriously his role as the devoted dog who greets his master when he returns home from school. In recent years, I have played up the gag that he doesn't even remember his master's name, but simply thinks of him as "that round-headed kid."

One of the questions most frequently asked of a cartoonist seems to be: "Where do you get your ideas?" After twenty-five years of drawing the *Peanuts* comic strip, I feel that I have learned a good deal about creativity and how one prepares an idea. Still rather a mystery to me is where some of the little phrases come from, and why it is possible to think of ten ideas in one day, and not be able to think of a single one the next. Perhaps I would be better off simply saying that I don't know how I think of all these ideas, which would be the same kind of answer I frequently give people who say, "I just want to let you know how much I admire your philosophy." This is a statement that continually baffles me, for I sincerely do not know what they mean. Therefore, all I can do is say "Thank you." I am always tempted, however, to start some kind of discussion to find out just what it is they really admire.

Some of my ideas can be traced back. I have drawn many cartoons showing the children standing in line to buy tickets to a movie, because my memories of Saturday afternoons at the Park Theater in St. Paul are so vivid. Almost nothing could prevent us from seeing the latest episode of this Saturday afternoon serial and the movie that followed. One day, the theater advertised that the first 500 customers would receive a free Butterfinger candy bar. I must have been the 501st child in line, because when I got up to the window, the man said, "Sorry, that's all there is." Forty years later, I had the same thing happen to Charlie Brown. The shape of the theater itself inspired another Sunday page. Charlie Brown is talking about how things change as we grow older. Of course I used his father as the instrument for my own recollections, and his father has apparently told him how the theater that he attended when he was a small boy seemed to get narrower and narrower as the years went by. This is similar to going back to a house where you once lived when you were young, and discovering that the backyard you remember as being so large is really absurdly small. Another time, Charlie Brown's father, also using my memory, recalls a cute little girl he used to know. When he picked her up in his 1934 black two-door sedan, she reached over and locked the driver's side of the car before he could get back around to his side of the car. She then sat there and grinned at him. These are the little jokes that make new love such a joy, and even though Peppermint Patty is not able to understand it, Charlie Brown instinctively knows that those moments should be cherished. Charlie Brown has also defined security as being able to sleep in the back seat of your parents' car. This, again, is a childhood memory, one supported by many readers who have told me that they also recall the wonderful joy of doing this with a feeling of complete security when returning home late at night. The shattering blow comes in later years when one realizes that this can never happen again. Adults are doomed to ride in the front seat forever.

Probably one of the biggest defeats any of us can experience in this life is being turned down by the girl we love, and then seeing her turn around and almost immediately marry someone else. This is a defeat from which it is almost impossible to recover. Charlie Brown's defeats, of course, are a caricature. None of us suffers the continual agony he does because his life is caricatured to the same degree that he is drawn. I have memories of a little girl, which have been translated into many defeats for Charlie Brown. He is talking in one particular page about an episode related to him and his family. It seems that his father and the girl had spent a wonderful day together having a picnic, and then going to a movie. The father tells how this movie had impressed him very much, and how afterward whenever he saw Anne Baxter in other films it would always take him back to that wonderful day he spent with the girl he loved. When telling a friend about it, however, the friend says, "Why, that was not Anne Baxter in the movie, it was Susan Hayward." This is how my own memories become mixed up with the memories of Charlie Brown's fictional father. For years, the sight of Anne Baxter on a late-late show or in a movie depressed me, for it brought back memories of that day, and that evening, and my defeat. And when someone told me that I had been depressed by the wrong fact all those years, it came as quite a shock.

Life has many finalities, and readers being able to make their own interpretations is, I suppose, what makes a cartoon idea successful. I frequently keep little scraps of paper in one of my desk drawers with slight notations for ideas that I hope someday to put together into a workable strip. One that I thought about for over a year eventually became one of the most sought-after pages I have ever done. We have received countless requests for the original and for reprints. It all started when my oldest son, Monte, was in high school and was involved with an art class where the project was a coat-hanger sculpture. He was telling me about it one day while we were riding home in the car from school, and he said that he was going to transform a coat hanger into the figure of a baseball pitcher. It sounded like a good idea to me, and I was anxious to hear about the final results. Several weeks went by before he mentioned it again, and this time he told me that the teacher had handed back the projects and he had received a C on his coat-hanger sculpture. I remember being quite disturbed by this, because I could not understand how a teacher was able to grade this kind of project. I thought about it as the months went by, and finally translated it into the Sunday page where Sally expresses indignation over receiving the same grade for her piece of coat-hanger sculpture. Her questions were the same ones that I wanted to ask Monte's teacher. Had he judged the sculpture as a piece of art? If so, what criteria did he use to judge it? Was he grading the person on his ability to create this work of art? If so, what control did the person have over the talent that was given him at birth? Was the person being graded upon what he had learned in the project? If so, should the teacher not be willing to share in the grade? Sally made a good instrument for this kind of idea, for she is a character who expresses indignation well, and who is completely puzzled by all of the things she has to go through in school.

This, of course, is one of the secrets to casting a comic strip. It is much like casting a drama company, where you must have actors who can play whatever roles are called for. The comic strip itself should have a variety of personalities so that you are not always striking the same note. You must have a full keyboard on which to play out the themes and variations demanded each day. Lucy has been inviting Charlie Brown to come running up to kick the football and then pulling it away each year for eighteen years. Every time I complete this annual page, I am sure I will never be able to think of another one, but so far I have always managed to come up with a new twist for the finish. (I suppose I have been encouraged to keep it up during the last three or four years because California's ex-governor, Ronald Reagan, once told me that this was one of his favorite episodes, and I am easily flattered into continuing something if I have been told that it has been a favorite.) It all started, of course, with a childhood memory of being unable to resist the temptation to pull away the football at the kickoff. We all did it, we all fell for it. In fact, I was told by a professional football player that he actually saw it happen in a college game at the University of Minnesota. The Gophers were apparently leading by a good margin, everyone was enjoying himself, and the man holding the football, like the kids in the neighborhood, could not resist the temptation to pull it away. I wish I had been there to see it.

I have never been a very successful kite flyer and have used the excuse that I never lived where there were good areas to fly them. When I was growing up, we always lived in residential areas that had too many trees and too many telephone wires. Recollections of those handicaps inspired Charlie Brown's troubles with kite flying. As I grew older and tried to fly kites for my own children, I discovered that I still had the same problems. I observed that when a kite becomes caught in a tall tree, it is irretrievable and gradually disappears over a period of several weeks. Now obviously the kite had to go someplace, so it seemed to me that the tree must be eating it. This is how the series developed about Charlie Brown's violent battles with his local "kite-eating tree."

When my daughter Amy had her fifteenth birthday, I gave her a dozen roses and told her that she would soon be a beautiful young lady and that the boys would be calling on her and probably would be bringing her presents. I told her that I wanted to be the first one in her life to give her a dozen roses. This was the inspiration for the Sunday page that showed Peppermint Patty receiving roses from her father on her birthday. For several years, I have referred to our youngest daughter, Jill, as a "rare gem," so I simply combined our two daughters into one and created the very sentimental page that concludes with Peppermint Patty saying, "Suddenly, I feel very feminine."

I suppose my long-time interest in music enabled me to carry out the ideas involving Schroeder playing his toy piano. This interest was kept alive by several of my friends at Art Instruction. We all collected classical albums, which we frequently shared on evenings when we got together to listen to music and challenge each other in wild games of hearts. Having been fascinated for several months by Strauss waltzes, I graduated one day to the purchase of Beethoven's Second Symphony, and I remember that this record opened up a whole new world for me.

A toy piano that we had bought for our oldest daughter, Meredith, eventually became the piano that Schroeder uses for his daily practicing. Seeing a portion of Beethoven's Ninth Symphony in print gave me the idea for the many episodes involving Schroeder's admiration for that great composer. I have been asked many times: "Why

Beethoven?" The answer is simply that it is funnier that way. There are certain words and names that work better than others. I don't believe it would be half as funny if Schroeder admired Brahms. There is also the very practical fact that to most of us laymen, Beethoven, Rembrandt, and Shakespeare are the three mountain poets in music, art, and literature. I have read several biographies of Beethoven—being strangely fascinated by the lives of composers, much more so than by the lives of painters—and from these biographies have managed to come up with different things that have concerned Schroeder. For a long time I had thought that the sentence "Lobkow-itz stopped his annuity" was an extremely funny sentence, and I was happy to find a way to use it. Sometimes, drawing the musical scores that Schroeder plays can be very tedious, but I love the pattern that the notes make on the page. I have always tried to be authentic in this matter. I believe that some readers enjoy trying to determine what it is that Schroeder is playing.

Linus's blanket was inspired by the blankets that our first three children dragged around the house, and the character of "Joe Cool," as expressed through Snoopy, evolved out of something that my second son, Craig, mentioned when I overheard a conversation between him and some other teenagers at our ice arena. Craig is also the inspiration for one of the more recent series involving "Joe Motocross."

My son Monte claims to have been the one who gave me the idea for Snoopy chasing the Red Baron in his World War I flying gear while atop his "Sopwith Camel" doghouse. I, of course, deny that he actually gave me the idea, but I will admit that he inspired it, for at the time he was very much involved with building plastic models of World War I airplanes. It was on an afternoon when he was showing me one of his models that I drew a helmet on Snoopy and placed him in a pilot's pose on top of his doghouse. The whole thing kind of fit together. You might say it simply took off, and I knew I had one of the best things I had thought of in a long time. In fact, this theme went on for several years and even produced two separate books.

Direct ideas have been much more rare. Our youngest daughter, Jill, came up to me one day and said, "I just discovered something. If you hold your hands upside down, you get the opposite of what you pray for." I used this as an idea exactly as she said it. Craig also told me one day that a good way to clean one's fingernails was to use toothpaste. Again, I used the idea almost the way he said it. Another time our second daughter, Amy, provided me with an idea that I think came out as well as any I have ever drawn. The entire family was around the dinner table and, for some reason, Amy seemed particularly noisy that evening. After putting up with this for about ten minutes, I turned to her and said, "Amy, couldn't you be quiet for just a little while?" She said nothing, but picked up a piece of bread and began to butter it with a knife and asked, "Am I buttering too loud for you?" This was very easily translated into a Linus and Lucy Sunday page.

In going through hundreds of Sunday pages that I have drawn over the years, I was startled to discover that the year 1968 produced a sudden turn in new ideas. For some reason, I was able to come up with a whole flock of new themes that I had never worked on before. I have looked back to that year, but have been unable to discover what it might have been that caused me to be able to think of so many new ideas at the time. Generally speaking, it seems that more good cartoon ideas have come out of a mood of sadness than a feeling of well-being. A couple of years ago, some events in my life saddened me to such a degree that I could no longer listen to the car radio. I did not want to risk becoming depressed while riding alone in the car, and I found that almost everything I listened to on the car radio would send me into a deep depression. In spite of this, I was still able to come up with cartoon ideas that were not only as good as anything I had ever done, but carried the strip forward into new areas.

At another earlier time, I had an album of Hank Williams songs to which I used to listen over and over. One night, saddened by the plaintive lyrics of lost love, I created the first of a long series where

Charlie Brown tried so desperately to get up the courage to speak to the little red-haired girl. It would be difficult to explain to someone how a Hank Williams song had prompted such thoughts, but this is the way it happened.

Not all of my ideas have worked out successfully. One day, while searching for some kind of new story to work on, I decided to have the character named Frieda, the little girl who is so proud of her naturally curly hair, threaten Snoopy with bringing a cat into the neighborhood. Snoopy was horrified and, when the cat arrived, did not like it at all. Fortunately for him, I also discovered that *I* didn't care much for the cat. For one thing, I realized that I don't draw a cat very well, and secondly, if I were to keep up the relationship, I would have a traditional cat-and-dog strip, which was something I certainly wanted to avoid. The cat and the dog could not talk to each other because Snoopy never talks, he only thinks. So I would have had to show the cat and dog thinking to each other, which was totally unreasonable. More important, the cat brought Snoopy back to being too much of a real dog. By the time the cat had come into the strip, Snoopy was drifting further and further into his fantasy life, and it was important that he continue in that direction. To take him back to his earlier days would not work, so I did the obvious and removed the cat. (My only regret was that I had named the cat after Faron Young, a country-and-western singer whom I admired very much. This was the second time that a country-and-western singer had contributed something to the strip.) An offstage cat now works better than a real one in the same way that the little red-haired girl, Linus's blanket-hating grandmother, Charlie Brown's father, the barber, and the kids' teachers all work better in the reader's imagination. There comes a time when it is actually too late to draw these offstage characters. I would never be able to draw the little red-haired girl, for example, as well as the reader draws her in his imagination.

The early years of *Peanuts* contain many ideas that revolved around very tiny children, because my own children were still young at the time. As the strip grew, it took on a slight degree of

sophistication, although I have never claimed to be the least sophisticated myself. But it also took on a quality that I think is even more
important, and that is one which I can only describe as abstraction.
The neighborhood in which the characters lived ceased gradually
to be real. Snoopy's doghouse could function only if it were drawn
from a direct side view. Snoopy himself had become a character so
unlike a dog that he could no longer inhabit a real doghouse. And
the cartooning of the other characters, with their large, round heads
and tiny arms, came frequently to prohibit them from doing some
of the more realistic things that a more normal style of cartooning
would allow. Nevertheless, this was the direction I wanted to take,
and I believe it has led me to do some things that no one ever before
attempted in a comic strip.

There are many standard poses that I use in the *Peanuts* drawings, and they are all used for definite reasons, some more important
than others. I was always overly cautious with my own children, wor-
rying constantly of their becoming injured, or worse, in some mis-
hap. When I began to draw the kids in the strip talking to each other,
the obvious pose was to show them sitting on the curb, reminiscent
of the early "Skippy" strips, drawn by Perey Crosby. The characters in
Peanuts, however, were much younger than Skippy and his friends,
and I was always sensitive about showing them sitting on a street
curb, where they could very easily get run over. Therefore, I always
drew them sitting at the end of the front walk that ran down from the
steps, out to the main sidewalk. This was not always a suitable pose
for some of the later strips, so I eventually changed it to show them
standing by a stone wall. This gave the reader a chance to speculate as
to what the characters might be looking at while talking about life's
problems and leaning in various positions. I also gradually became
aware that it was important for readers instantly to identify the characters and what they were doing. This is the main reason I have never
gone in for using tricky camera angles and a variety of poses from
panel to panel. For example, there would be no advantage to show
Schroeder from a variety of views. It is much more important that

the reader identify him immediately and have the feeling of familiarity as he sees him seated at his tiny toy piano. Admittedly, it would be difficult to draw some of these characters from different angles. In certain cases, they simply do not fit, and other poses are easier to fake from certain angles. When it comes right down to it, we have to get back to what looks best, and Schroeder looks best when drawn from side view, playing his piano. Also, I have always drawn the characters viewed from their own level, which gets the reader right down into the picture without any superior, adult view. I probably am the only cartoonist who always draws grass from side view.

The more Snoopy moved into his life of fantasy, the more important it became for his doghouse to remain in side view. You simply cannot have a dog doing and thinking the things that Snoopy does on a realistic doghouse. The image is much more acceptable when the doghouse is drawn only from the side. When necessary, it almost loses its identity completely. Snoopy's typewriter could never balance on the peak the way it does and, of course, Snoopy is somewhat of a mystery when one examines his sleeping pose closely. I once inquired of a veterinarian how birds stay on tree limbs when they fall asleep. He told me that their claws receive a message from their brain after they have fallen asleep, which tightens a certain muscle, keeping them from tumbling off the branch. He said a similar thing occurs to horses, allowing them to sleep while standing. Humans do not have this ability. When I am asked how Snoopy remains on top of his doghouse after falling asleep, I am now able to say that his brain sends a message to his ears, which lock him to the top of his doghouse.

The baseball scenes work wonderfully well even though we never see the other team. Most of the time we are focused on Charlie Brown, standing on top of the pitcher's mound. It was Robert Short, author of *The Gospel According to Peanuts*, who once reminded me that Charlie Brown's pose on the pitcher's mound was not unlike that of Job on his ash heap. He was quite surprised when I told him that this had never occurred to me.

Baseball has played a prominent role in the strip because it is effective when dealing with static situations. A violent sport, or one that contains a lot of action, does not lend itself to having characters standing around spouting philosophical opinions. There is also the element of tension, as in the sport of baseball itself. I can show Charlie Brown standing on the mound, and build up the tension of what is going to happen before the game begins or before he throws the next pitch. This would be difficult with almost any other sport.

The front-view pose of Linus holding his blanket is used for two reasons: again, for familiarity, and secondly, for practical reasons. With his large head and short arms, it would be very difficult to draw Linus sucking his thumb from side view, for he would have a hard time stretching his arm out that far. The animators in Hollywood, who have worked on our many television shows and movies, have discovered this much to their chagrin. There are some poses that simply have to be avoided.

The introduction of Woodstock into the strip is a good demonstration of how some things cannot work until they have been drawn properly. The little birds that had appeared earlier were drawn much too realistically to be able to fill humorous roles, but as I loosened up the drawing style, Woodstock gradually developed. A problem similar to that of the cat has now come about, and I have had to back off slightly. I would much prefer that Snoopy not communicate with Woodstock, but there are some ideas that are too important to abandon, so I have him speaking to Woodstock through "thought" balloons. I've held fast with Woodstock's means of communication, though it has been tempting at times to have him talk. I feel it would be a mistake to give in on this point, however, for I think it is more important that all of Woodstock's talking remain depicted simply in the little scratch marks that appear above his head.

If *Peanuts* has been unique in any way, it has been because of the absence of adults. I usually say that they do not appear because the daily strip is only an inch and a half high, and they wouldn't have room to stand up. Actually, they have been left out because they would intrude in a world where they could only be uncomfortable. Adults are not needed in the *Peanuts* strip. In earlier days I experimented with offstage voices, but soon abandoned this, as it was not only impractical but actually clumsy. Instead, I have developed a cast of offstage adults who are talked about, but never seen or heard. Charlie Brown's father seems to be a gentle soul who is developing a few problems. Charlie Brown once said that he saw him in the kitchen late one night looking at his high school annual, eating cold cereal, and looking very sad. This would say something about almost every one of us. Linus's blanket-hating grandmother has caused a good deal of trouble for poor Linus because she seems to be convinced that she can cure him of his terrible habit of having to drag around his spiritual blotter. When he knows that she is coming over to their house to visit, and realizing it is impossible to hide his blanket from her, he tucks it into a self-addressed envelope and drops it into the mail, knowing it will not come back for at least four or five days. Another strong character who never appears is Linus's teacher, Miss Othmar. Linus denies that he loves her, insisting he is simply "very fond of the ground on which she walks." I have often heard it said that children know a lot more about what is going on around them than adults are willing to admit. But I have also observed that children sometimes understand much less of what is going on around them than we think they do. For one thing, children seem to live more for themselves than do adults, and I see no reason why they should not. They frequently get a distorted view of what is actually happening. I pointed this out once in a little story about Linus and his teacher where he had been assigned to bring some eggshells to school for a project in which they were studying igloos. The eggshells were evidently to be placed in a setting where they would appear to be an Eskimo village. For some reason, Linus could not remember to bring the eggshells to school, and he noticed that Miss Othmar was very upset. Being very self-conscious, as most children are, he thought for sure that Miss Othmar was upset because of his inability to remember the eggshells. It turned out, however, that Miss

Othmar merely was involved in an after-hours romance. Eventually she ran off to get married.

I am not sure, but I believe that in addition to being the first cartoonist to use authentic musical scores in his comic strip, I am also the first to use extensive theological references. I have done this in spite of severe criticism from people who have written in to me saying that it is a desecration of the scriptures to quote them in "such a lowly thing as a newspaper comic strip." My mind reels with countless things I would like to write back to these people, but I always decide it is better not to say anything. These scriptural references have always been done with dignity and, of course, with much love, for I am extremely fond of studying both the Old and the New Testaments.

I received a letter one day from a young seminary student named Robert Short, who had been using some of the *Peanuts* material as part of his thesis. He asked permission to have his material published in book form. I appreciated many of the things he said in his thesis, though I realized that when dealing with religious opinions, you are leaving yourself open for all kinds of criticism and trouble. I told him that I would certainly be pleased if his book were published, but I wanted no one to think that we had collaborated on his work. This is my philosophy: Always accept the compliments and praise, but avoid the blame. As it turned out, *The Gospel According to Peanuts* was a tremendous best-seller and did much good. It opened the way for Bob to tour the country and speak to thousands of college students, as it opened the way in a similar manner for other religious workers to lead discussion groups.

While I have introduced many theological themes into *Peanuts*, I have also been aware that it is unfair to subscribing newspaper editors to promote views that can become too personal. I do believe, however, that it is quite possible to use the scriptures in a gentle manner in a comic strip. My own theological views have changed considerably over the past twenty-five years, and I now shy away from anyone who claims to possess all of the truth. I do not find it easy to discuss with an interviewer things of a spiritual nature, for they do not always come out on the printed page in a manner that can be easily understood. I find it much safer, as well as more gratifying, to reserve theological discussions for a time when you can look the other person directly in the eye. There are too many "howevers" that need to be spoken when discussing subjects this sensitive, and they simply do not come out well in the average magazine or newspaper interview.

Every profession and every type of work has its difficulties, and one of the most difficult aspects of creating a comic strip is attempting to sustain a certain quality of day-to-day schedule that never ends. Trying not only to maintain that level, but to improve the feature as the months go by, in spite of the problems one may be having in one's life, makes cartooning a very demanding profession. I believe the ability to sustain a certain quality, in spite of everything, is one of the elements that separates the good features from the weaker ones. I went through one strange phase in my life when I became quite disturbed by dreams, which occurred to me irregularly over a period of several weeks. I would find in my dreams that I was crying uncontrollably, and when I awakened, I was extremely depressed. Naturally, it is not easy to disregard something like this, to forget it all and start thinking of funny cartoons, for the daily pressures of life affect us all. I have talked to many people who have agreed that they find themselves feeling angry throughout much of the day. The mere routine of having to deal with customers or company people in superior positions is enough to make the working day difficult. Sometimes, simply reading the morning paper, or watching the television news, is enough to discourage anyone. We become angry with ourselves, with our family, our fellow workers, with people we meet in stores, and, of course, with the government. It takes a good deal of maturity to be able to set all this anger aside and carry on with your daily work.

Charles M. Schulz, *Peanuts Jubilee: My Life and Art with Charlie Brown and Others* (New York: Holt, Rinehart and Winston, 1975), 81–100.

But a Comic Strip
Has to Grow

Drawing a daily comic strip is not unlike having an English theme hanging over your head every day for the rest of your life. I was never very good at writing those English themes in high school, and I usually put them off until the last minute. The only thing that saves me in trying to keep up with a comic strip schedule is the fact that it is quite a bit more enjoyable.

I am really a comic strip fanatic and always have been. When I was growing up in St. Paul, Minnesota, we subscribed to both local newspapers and always made sure that we went to the drugstore on Saturday night to buy the Minneapolis Sunday papers so that we would be able to read every comic published in the area. At that time, I was a great fan of *Buck Rogers*, *Popeye*, and *Skippy*.

After high school, I had a job delivering packages around the downtown St. Paul area, and I used to enjoy walking by the windows of the St. Paul *Pioneer Press* and watching the Sunday comics as they came rolling off the presses. It was my dream, of course, that one day my own comic strip would be included.

Almost twenty years have gone by since I first began drawing Charlie Brown and Snoopy, and I find that I still enjoy drawing them as much as I ever did, but, strangely enough, one of my greatest joys is gaining an extra week on the schedule. I have walked away from the post office many times with a tremendous feeling of joy, knowing that I have mailed in six strips that I thought were really good and that I have gained a week on that oppressive schedule.

During these twenty years, I have had the opportunity to observe what makes a good comic strip. I am convinced that the ones that have survived and maintained a high degree of quality are those which have a format that allows the creator room to express every idea that comes to him. A comic strip should have a very broad keyboard and should certainly not be a one- or two-note affair. If you are going to survive, you simply have to make use of every thought and every experience which have come to you.

A comic strip also has to grow. The only way you can stay ahead of your imitators is to search out new territories. Also, what is funny in a comic strip today will not necessarily be funny the following week. A good example of this is the character of Snoopy. The mere fact that we could read Snoopy's thoughts was funny in itself when *Peanuts* first began. Now, of course, it is the content of those thoughts that is important, and as he progresses in his imagination to new personalities, some of the things which he originally did as an ordinary dog would no longer be funny. Snoopy's personality in the strip has to be watched very carefully, for it can get away from me. Control over such a character requires a certain degree of common sense. I also believe that a comic strip, like a novel, should introduce the reader to new areas of thought and endeavor; these areas should be treated in an authentic manner. I never draw about anything unless I feel that I have a better than average knowledge of my subject. This does not mean that I am an expert on Beethoven, kite-flying, or psychiatry, but it means that as a creative person, I have the ability to skim the surface of such subjects and use just what I need.

Many times people come up to me and tell me how much they appreciate the philosophy of *Peanuts*. This never fails to confuse me, for I really do not know what this philosophy is. It has always seemed to me that the strip has a rather bitter feeling to it, and it certainly deals in defeat. It has given me the opportunity to express many of my own thoughts about life and people. It is my own opinion that is absolutely necessary for each one of us to strive to gain emotional maturity. Unless a person becomes mature in all things, he will always have fears and anxieties plaguing him. It is interesting

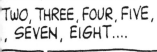

to put these adult fears into the conversations of the children in *Peanuts*. The passage of time is an area that will almost always show up a person's immaturity. Children have a strange attitude toward time, for they do not have the patience to wait for days to pass. They want what they want immediately, and adults who are incapable of learning to wait for things will find themselves in all sorts of trouble.

It is also immature not to be able to realize that things that are going to happen in the future are quite often inevitable. If children are allowed to do so, they will put off almost anything, merely because it is in the future; of course, adults will do the same.

I am asked quite frequently to attempt to analyze each of the characters in the strip, but I find myself incapable of doing this. I really cannot talk about Charlie Brown, Linus, or Lucy as individuals. I can draw them, and I can think of things for them to do, but I do not talk well about them.

One thing that does interest me, however, is the set of offstage characters I have gradually accumulated. A reader once wrote to me and gave a fairly good description of what he thought Peppermint Patty's father must be like. This offstage parent refers to his daughter as a "rare gem," and apparently tolerates her tomboyishness quite well. The reader speculated that the father has either divorced his wife or perhaps she has died. I have treated Charlie Brown's father in a fair amount of detail, because I have let it be known that he is very receptive to his son's impromptu visits to the barber shop. Most of this is autobiographical, for my dad always greeted me cordially when I would drop in at his barbershop, and I used to go there and sit and read the newspapers and magazines until he closed his shop in the evening. He also never objected if I rang the NO SALE button on the cash register and removed a nickel for a candy bar.

Linus's mother seems to be the peculiar one. As Charlie Brown once remarked, "I am beginning to understand why you drag that blanket around." She seems to be obsessed with his doing well in school, and tries to spur him on by sneaking notes into his lunch which read, "Study hard today. Your father and I are very proud of you and want you to get a good education."

Some of the offstage characters reach a point where they could never be drawn. I think the little redheaded girl is a lot like the inside of Snoopy's doghouse. Each of us can imagine what she must look like much better than I could ever draw her, and I am sure that every reader sees a different doghouse interior and would be a little disappointed if I were to attempt to draw it in detail.

Linus's beloved Miss Othmar, his teacher, is a rather strange person, and I have tried to do much with her through the conversation of Linus. I have experimented with a two-level story line at times. I have tried to show Linus's view of what is happening at school, but then show what actually was occurring. I have done this to bring out a truth I have observed, and this is that children see more than we think they do, but at the same time almost never seem to know what is going on. This is an interesting paradox, and one with which adults should try to acquaint themselves, if they are going to deal well with children.

I am very proud of the comic strip medium and am never ashamed to admit that I draw a comic strip. I do not regard it as great art, but I have always felt it is certainly on the level with other entertainment mediums which are part of the so-called "popular arts." In many ways, I do not think we have realized the potential of the comic strip, but sometimes I feel it is too late. Many regard the comic page as a necessary evil and a nuisance, but it is there and it helps sell newspapers. With a little more tolerance and with a little more dedication on the part of those who create the comics, perhaps we could do better. I look back upon great features such as *Out Our Way*, and I feel that perhaps we can never recapture some of that glory. I really shudder when I read a description of a new feature about to be launched by some syndicate and they refer to it as "off-beat." It is time we have some new features which are "on-beat," and which are about real people doing real things.

Charles M. Schulz, "But a Comic Strip Has to Grow," *Saturday Review*, April 12, 1969, 73–74.

What Do You Do with a Dog That Doesn't Talk?

omic-strip characters, I have noticed after 30 years of drawing *Peanuts*, come and go quickly. Some work better than others. Some don't work at all. Some, like Snoopy, are so strong that they tend, if you let them, to take over the strip. Others, like Frieda, with the naturally curly hair, drop by the wayside, either because they do not inspire enough things that are funny, or because the artist has outgrown them. But the turnover is still nowhere near as great, I'm happy to be able to say, as it is with the characters in your average television series.

Television is a tyrannical kind of medium. Even when you are making an animated cartoon out of my characters, as Bill Melendez

and I have been doing for more than 15 years now. You don't have a captive audience the way you do in a movie or play. In TV, you're at the mercy of some guy in a chair. You can't try the show out in New Haven, then write a new second act. If the viewer doesn't instantly like what he sees, it's *zap!* off with your head while he tunes in something else. There's no way you can say to him, "Hey, wait, there's this *great number* coming up in a minute." You have to grab 'em right now.

This is difficult because the grabbiest characters I have are not necessarily the ones that work best on television. Snoopy doesn't even talk. In the strip he communicates by means of thought balloons. Woodstock merely peeps. One has to imagine what he is actually saying. As much as I love pantomime, it severely limits what you can do in film with two of the characters who are mainstays of the strip. All that poetry, Snoopy philosophizing on top of the doghouse, Woodstock dreaming impossible dreams, etc., doesn't sustain itself in film, even if you could figure out how to do it. In its place we all too often substitute action: a boat race, a figure-skating competition, a spelling bee, complete with conventional bad guys. That's fine except the story tends to fall into cliché. But it gives new impetus to the characters who *can* talk. And it makes a star all over again out of Charlie Brown.

Charlie Brown is indeed one of the good guys, which for a comic strip is just right. Some comic-strip heroes survive simply by being what they are. That's Charlie Brown. Others by being quotable. Thurber characters do that. People remember things said in Thurber cartoons from 25 years ago. Can anybody remember anything Mickey Mouse ever said? Mickey and Charlie Brown survived by merely being there.

This is largely true of all comic-strip heroes. Invariably they are small and put-upon, and they never get to say the funny things themselves. Pogo was a likable little possum. Mickey was a kind of elder-statesman Mouse. Charlie Brown, for all his nagging insecurities, was and is the voice of reason, really very low-key in relation to the others. Yet he holds the whole thing together.

Another thing I find bothersome about television is that it dictates what you can and can't do. A novel allows time to dig beneath the surface and develop character. A comic strip, strangely enough, affords a similar luxury: even though it takes only 16 seconds a day to read, cumulatively it goes on forever. Big changes naturally evolve over the years. Snoopy, for example, was just a cuddly puppy of the most conventional sort when *Peanuts* began. When he got up on the doghouse and began to fantasize, he became something very different. In television it is difficult even to carry on a conversation, let alone philosophize.

Not that it can't be challenging. Really nice moments happen. I remember how I agonized over the spelling-bee show. In the end Charlie Brown loses and is so depressed that he goes to bed, swearing that he will never get up and play baseball again. A flat ending. I needed something. I thought about it a long time. Then it hit me. Linus opens the door and asks to come in. "I don't care what you do," says Charlie Brown glumly.

"So you feel bad about the spelling bee? Let everybody down, did you? But did you notice, Charlie Brown, the world didn't come to an end?" says Linus. So Charlie Brown gets up, gets dressed, goes out, and everybody is playing marbles and the world is going on. I liked it.

The problem in television is one of translation, making it work in another medium. Whatever you do, you put a lot of yourself into it. For instance, my children are growing up and moving away and I find myself missing them and wishing they'd stay closer to home. This leads to the gloomy thought that I am growing older. I instinctively know this idea is going to find its way into the strip. But how?

I decide it will be funny to have Lucy complain about getting old. It will also ease my own fears about it. Or at least give them voice. But I have to find just the right person for Lucy to complain to. It turns out to be Schroeder. So I have Lucy peer soulfully up at him, sitting at his piano playing Beethoven, as disdainful of girls as ever.

"Will you love me when I'm old and crabby?" she demands.

"I don't love you now so how can I love you then?" he replies without missing a note.

That idea makes for a strip. I may get four or five more on the same theme. Or I may get none. Or I may have to throw one away, as I did in this particular case. It showed Lucy fiercely resisting, simply refusing to grow old. A funny notion, I thought. But for some reason it was flat; it didn't express what was happening. So I mentally file it away and go on to another or the next.

People speculate that I am Charlie Brown. Well, maybe. But only in the sense that all my characters reflect some aspect of me. Charlie Brown is the gentle, accepting part, a "loser" in name only. Lucy is the part that's capable of saying mean, sarcastic things. Lucy could not be a male. When she says, "Hey, stupid Beagle!" or pulls the football on Charlie Brown, we can accept it from a little girl. It's nice to have someone who can do that; there's not much meanness in the strip. Yet Lucy has her soft, vulnerable side. When Lucy's world goes sour and Linus tells her, "You still have a little brother who loves you," she breaks down and cries.

Linus, my serious side, is the house intellectual, bright, well-informed—which, I suppose, may contribute to his feelings of insecurity. He lets himself be bamboozled by Lucy. In recent years I have drifted away from the whole business of Linus's blanket. Maybe because my children have grown older—and no longer need it. Other characters—Peppermint Patty, Marcie, Sally, Woodstock—seem to have persuaded him.

Peppermint Patty, the tomboy, is forthright, doggedly loyal, with a devastating singleness of purpose, the part of us that goes through life with blinders on. This can be wonderful at times but also disastrous. Patty was never very smart. Then one day Marcie appeared. Marcie is devoted to her, calls her "Sir" and doesn't mind following her around, which is deceptive. Marcie is one-up on Patty in every way. She sees the truth of things, where it invariably escapes Patty. I like Marcie.

Schroeder? Well, in the first year I needed a baby. My own children were very small. I'd just bought a toy piano for my daughter Meredith. He had to do something so I had him grow up quickly and play Beethoven. Out of this came the business of Lucy lounging on the piano. This is a parody of women falling for musicians, and your old Aunt who warned, "Never fall in love with a trumpet player."

Schroeder invariably rejects Lucy. The more he does, the more passionate her ardor.

Sally, on the other hand, is the complete pragmatist. I personally do not like her; she is rude to her big brother Charlie. I could easily become angry with her. Yet there is a certain charm when she fractures the language: "By golly, if any centimeters come in this room, I'll *step* on them!"

Molly Volley is at once an off-shoot of my own recent involvement in tennis and a caricature of human behavior on the court. She is one tough cookie who embodies the widely held American belief that the only thing that matters is winning. Molly doesn't actually cheat; she just shades the call a little. She doesn't fly her private jet to the tournament the way golfer Arnold Palmer does. You think champions are made at Wimbledon? They're made out there on some remote, windswept, backcountry tournament where nobody's watching and nobody cares. Charlie Brown is appalled by her conduct. I can empathize with her.

Spike, Snoopy's brother, is a beautiful example of images evoked by a location: we know he lives with the coyotes outside Needles, and that's about all we know. There is about him, with his thin, faintly exotic mustache and soulful eyes, an air of mystery that is totally foreign to what Snoopy is. Our imagination takes over.

Not so with Snoopy. Snoopy's rich fantasy life is all too specific. He becomes the Famous Author or World War I Flying Ace in his Sopwith Camel cursing the Red Baron and not really treating Charlie Brown, who feeds him every night, very well. Snoopy has gone way beyond Charlie Brown. Only Woodstock can really keep up.

Woodstock came out of nowhere. Originally he was not a male. He was one of two undifferentiated little birdies born in a nest on the top of Snoopy's stomach. The sequence involved Snoopy's worry about how long they would have to remain there. Even when they start to learn to fly, they flutter unsteadily back into the nest.

Well, somehow Woodstock, as yet unnamed, seemed to want to stick around. He became Snoopy's secretary, presumably female.

Then, when it came time to name "her," it seemed better that she be a he. He became Woodstock, after the festival.

Woodstock suggests something else to me. Next to, say, the majestic flight of the wild geese flying overhead when he and Snoopy go camping, Woodstock knows that he is very small and inconsequential indeed. It's a problem we all have. The universe boggles us. In the larger scheme, we suddenly realize, we amount to very little. It's frightening. Only a certain maturity will make us able to cope. The minute we abandon the quest for it we leave ourselves open to tragic results. Woodstock is a lighthearted expression of that idea.

As I said earlier, the strip is the mother lode. My reservations about television are that all too little of this kind of low-key poetry finds its way into the script. In television we tend to settle for the easy way out. It's like Linus explaining to Charlie Brown that when a kid gets to be 18 it's time for him to leave home.

"Even if it's a Sunday?" Charlie Brown says.

Television, too, will have to grow up. Even if it's a Sunday.

Charles M. Schulz, "What Do You Do with a Dog That Doesn't Talk?" *TV Guide*, February 23, 1980, 22–24.

"IN THE BOOK OF LIFE,
THE ANSWERS ARE NOT IN THE BACK!"

Charlie Brown

APPENDIX

Pale Horse, Pale Rider
by Katherine Anne Porter

Seven young men took part in the assassination plot that destroyed
the life of the Archduke Ferdinand, and hurled the nations into the
monstrous conflict we call World War I. All seven of these young
men were ill with tuberculosis. It has been said that fever has a way
of coloring one's view, and in their case it helped drive them toward
what they believed to be an heroic end. Another disease brought
fever and death to millions of people by the time the great conflict
was over, for an epidemic of influenza went around the world taking
its toll from all classes, races, and ages. The origin of the 1918 pan-
demic of influenza is shrouded in obscurity. Some medical authorities doubt that a single starting point ever existed. As early as 1916–
1917 numerous cases of "purulent bronchitis" were observed among
the British troops at a base in France. This outbreak was considered
to be somewhat dependent on the exceptionally cold weather of that
period. The earliest recorded outbreak in the United States seems to
have been at Camp Funston in Kansas, although the general belief
was that it had started in Boston and worked its way across the
country. The last-arriving American troops in France quickly spread
the disease through the A.E.F. The troopship *Leviathan* docked on a
particular day at Brest with ten thousand men aboard, four thousand of them stricken. At Camp Pontanezen in France, out of sixty-
five thousand soldiers, twelve thousand were down with the flu at
the same time. Americans in this camp were dying at the rate of two

hundred and fifty per day. By the time the epidemic was over in 1919, twenty million people in all parts of the world had died following influenza infection.

In *Pale Horse, Pale Rider* twenty-four year old Miranda, writer for a newspaper, becomes aware of a "burning slow headache" as she is taking her morning bath. She remembers "she had waked up with it and it had in fact begun the evening before." Fever colors Miranda's view of the next few days, and we are presented also with a series of her dreams which serve in a remarkable way to take us along the paths of torment she is to suffer.

Although Miranda and Adam, the soldier in the story, refer to them as part of an old negro hymn, the pale horse and the pale rider in the novel are the figures mentioned in the Sixth Chapter of the Book of Revelations. "When he opened the fourth seal, I heard the voice of the fourth living creature say, 'Come!' And I saw, and behold, a pale horse, and its rider's name was Death, and Hades followed him, and they were given power over a fourth of the earth, to kill with sword and with famine and with pestilence and by wild beasts of the earth." This rider brings not meaningless destruction, but destruction which serves the purpose of the justice of God. He is what we might call a divine administrator. One quarter of the earth is to feel his power so that the remainder might witness the events and thus be led to repent. In the Goodspeed translation of the New Testament the horse is described as being the "color of ashes." Moffatt claims it is "livid." Other translations call it "greenish yellow" which may account for the description of the stranger in the first dream in the opening passages of the novel.

In this dream, Miranda is in her room in the great farm house where she grew up. She is anxious to arise before the rest of the family in order to avoid entanglements which are only hinted at. She is aware of Death, "that lank greenish stranger" who hangs about the place, and she chooses to try to outrun him on horseback. The dream takes on nightmarish qualities as the stranger rides easily alongside her regarding her with a stare that indicates he can bide his time. She awakes as she shouts to him to ride on. "She is not going with him this time!" This is a dream of ill omen, and it suggests some of the troubles to come.

Most of the action in the novel takes place between the first and second dreams. Miranda is finding it difficult to cope with the problems faced by women during wartime. She lives on a very meager salary, and is pestered by committeemen who insist that she dedicate a portion of that salary towards the purchase of a Liberty bond. She has become very fond of a young officer named Adam who is from Texas. Like all soldiers he is living an intermission, and rather enjoys speculating about his chances of surviving in combat. For Adam, who is on leave, the days are free of responsibility, but for Miranda everything seems terribly wrong. They go for many walks together, and on one of these walks they view three different funerals passing by. Miranda begins to feel only "half awake." The disease that has moved around the world has descended upon her. "She wanted to say, 'Adam, come out of your dream and listen to me. I have pains in my chest and my head and my heart and they're real. I am in pain all over, and you are in such danger as I can't bear to think about, and why can we not save each other?'"

Miranda's second dream gives us an indication of the extent of her illness. She dreams of being in the cold mountains in the snow. This changes suddenly to a desire for warmth, and then the peaceful scenes of all the rivers she had ever known. But this is interrupted by the sight of a tall sailing ship with a gangplank running down to the foot of her bed. A slight sense of fear creeps over her as she notices a jungle behind the ship. Nevertheless, she runs down the gangplank, boards the ship, and is able to observe herself lying in bed. She sails off into the jungle, and is finally awakened by jungle noises which turn into words that cry, "danger, danger, danger" and "war, war, war." Adam and her landlady are arguing about Miranda's remaining in the apartment.

Adam risks his own health by staying to care for her. This accounts partially for his entering her dreams for the first time in her third recorded dream. She is in a small green wood that contains "inhuman concealed voices singing sharply like the whine of arrows." She sees Adam struck by these "singing arrows." He falls back, rises unwounded, is struck again and rises unwounded once more. Miranda attempts to block the flight of arrows with her own body, and as they pass through her heart, they continue on through his body. This third time he falls, but does not rise. She awakens screaming, and we have learned of the great depth of her feelings for Adam.

Her fourth dream is full of hospital images. Whiteness and silence, tall shadows moving behind a wide screen of sheets spread upon a frame, dark figures bowing, speechless figures in white, and a pallid white fog floating before her eyes. The seriousness of her illness is brought out by the torment of her dreams as it continues with the image of two white-clad executioners "pushing between them with marvelously deft and practical hands" a helpless old man who pleads for his life. The one doctor whom she met before being taken away in the ambulance, Dr. Hildesheim, becomes a hideous figure, a skull beneath a German helmet, and he is carrying an infant impaled on a bayonet which he throws into a well along with a pot of poison. The well is one she remembers from her father's farm, and again she awakens screaming.

She is now delirious when awake, and sees the nurse's hands as white tarantulas.

The fifth and final dream moves her closer toward death. Her internal torment is made up of words like "oblivion," eternity," and a "pit that is bottomless." Images of childhood are recalled to help turn away the call of death. Then, a stubborn will to live enters her dream. She is taken to a landscape of sea and sand. A great company of human beings, all the living she has ever known, comes toward her. She moves among them in a great "quietude of her ecstasy." Suddenly, a tremor of apprehension is felt. She has lost something, but she doesn't know what it is. "We have forgotten the dead, oh, the dead, where are they?" This time she awakens with the smell of death in her own body.

Miranda lives. One morning she finds herself waking from a dreamless sleep to hear the sound of bells, horns, and whistles. The war is over! There were no radios to spread the news. It got around slowly, but gradually spread along the Eastern seaboard and then westward. President Wilson issued the statement: "The Armistice was signed this morning. Everything for which America fought has been accomplished. It will now be our fortunate duty to assist by example." Miranda goes through the mail that has accumulated by her beside during her month's stay in the hospital, and finds a letter from a friend of Adam informing her that Adam has died of influenza while in camp. The pale rider has done his work.

Unpublished typescript dated May 24, 1965.

A Poem for Jeannie

You hurried by
    and caught my eye
And love sat near

"My name is Jeannie"
    "I'm so glad that you like me"
And the square at Ghirardelli
    and love moved closer

Can two people kiss
    In the sun among the crowd
While others pay no mind
    and love moves closer?

You hurried by
    and caught my eye
And love joined us forever.

Index